HOW TO TALK TO YOUR TEEN
ABOUT ANYTHING

HOW TO TALK TO YOUR TEEN ABOUT ANYTHING

EFFECTIVE COMMUNICATION STRATEGIES TO CONNECT WITH YOUR TEEN

KATIE MALINSKI, LCSW-S

ROCKRIDGE
PRESS

For general information on our other products and services or to obtain technical support, please contact our Customer Care Department within the United States at (866) 744-2665, or outside the United States at (510) 253-0500.

Rockridge Press publishes its books in a variety of electronic and print formats. Some content that appears in print may not be available in electronic books, and vice versa.

TRADEMARKS: Rockridge Press and the Rockridge Press logo are trademarks or registered trademarks of Callisto Media Inc. and/or its affiliates, in the United States and other countries, and may not be used without written permission. All other trademarks are the property of their respective owners. Rockridge Press is not associated with any product or vendor mentioned in this book.

Interior and Cover Designer: Michael Cook
Art Producer: Meg Baggott
Editor: Jed Bickman
Production Editor: Ruth Sakata Corley
Production Manager: Martin Worthington

All images used under license by Shutterstock
Author photo courtesy of Travis Miller

Paperback ISBN: 978-1-63807-447-2
eBook ISBN: 978-1-63807-596-7
R0

■ ▪ ■ ▪

This book is dedicated to my many teachers:
Mama, Maggie & Caroline, Travis,
friends, colleagues, and the clients who have
shared their stories with me over the years.
The good stuff in this book comes from
your love and generosity.

CONTENTS

INTRODUCTION

I was a therapist for kids, teens, and families for several years before I had my own kids, but motherhood was life-changing for me, personally and professionally. Parenting is hard, and although I had support as I entered motherhood, it still kicked my ass. Becoming a parent caused a major shift in my understanding of myself and my work as a therapist.

My big professional moment of realization was that I had the wrong person in the room; I had been seeing kids and teens, but becoming a parent helped me realize that *parents* need as much help and support as kids and teens, if not more. I revamped my practice, so that when parents inquired about putting their child into therapy, I asked if they would like to come in themselves first, to see if I could help their child through them. Although I am still a huge proponent of therapy for adults and children, supporting parents with their parenting has become my specialty, and I love my work.

If you feel lost or frustrated in communicating with your teenager, you aren't alone. I stumbled upon a funny example of this as I was finishing this book. I sent a rough draft of one chapter to a mom who had generously shared a story of a conflict with her teenager for one of my "Real-Life Scenarios." I changed details on all of the stories in order to protect the privacy of the families. Well, some time had elapsed since she told me her story, and I forgot to tell her the fictional names I'd given to her character. She wrote me back and said that she couldn't tell which scenario was hers, because she had lived them all. You are truly in good company.

My goal with this book is to offer support to parents of teenagers in a concrete way that's both accessible and flexible. Individual parent coaching and therapy are great, but they can be challenging to access, whether due to scheduling or financial obstacles. In this book, however, you can "take me with you" and get parent coaching on demand. *How to Talk with Your Teen about Anything* is here to help you strengthen fundamental communication skills, effectively communicate with your teenager, and improve your overall relationship. I'll also add one last, tiny, modest goal: I believe parents shape the future, and it's my hope that everything we do to raise this generation with compassion and attunement will do nothing less than change the world.

HOW TO USE THIS BOOK

How to Talk with Your Teen about Anything is organized around five core communication skills:

- Active Listening: the skill of putting energy and intention into your listening. It involves prioritizing the speaker, noticing explicit and implicit cues, suspending judgment, and signaling your attention.

- Authentic Communication: the skill of knowing and communicating your deepest truth. Authenticity increases communication effectiveness and strengthens relationships.

- Nonverbal Communication: the skill of being aware of the messages that the body sends. The message of a person's words can be strengthened, weakened, or even negated with facial expressions, posture, body position, tone of voice, and gestures.

- Emotional Regulation: the skill of recognizing and managing different "states" of the brain. Understanding and respecting the state of your teen's brain in challenging situations is a transformational parenting tool.

◆ Emotional Boundaries: the skill of recognizing and respecting the line between your emotions and your teen's emotions. Healthy emotional boundaries facilitate good communication.

Each of these topics are explored through a whole chapter of examples, discussion, practical advice, and an exercise or quiz to clarify or apply the concepts. The five core communication skills are each valuable on their own, but the combination of these is where you really get the magic.

Keep in mind that this book does not include advice related to severe problems like anxiety, depression, addiction, or other mental health diagnoses. Although the core techniques in this book can be a great adjunct to professional intervention, diagnosed mental-health challenges should be addressed by a licensed professional.

I truly hope this book helps you understand why communication becomes so difficult during the teen years and gives you concrete strategies and advice to improve your communication and your relationship with your teenager.

CHAPTER 1

THE ABCs OF PARENTING TEENS

If you're parenting a teenager, it's likely that you have more than a decade's worth of experience in this parenting gig. And yet, 10 or 15 years in, not only is the job still challenging, but it's challenging in new ways. The lessons you learned and the tools that were once effective don't seem to work anymore. Plus, the outside world is pressing in; teens are exploring their identity and their sexuality, and parents often feel anxious, vulnerable, and frustrated. Nevertheless, crafting new parenting skills that balance independence, structure, support, and companionship for your teen *is* possible. Indeed, more than possible, it's *necessary* for both your child's eventual "launch" and the quality of the relationship you get to enjoy with them in their adulthood. Chapter 1 begins with information about the changing role of the parent and the teen, as well as some of the struggles of parenting teens. This chapter includes a real-life scenario about enforcing household responsibilities, and closes with a discussion about the varying things that teens want, from life and from their parents.

BEING A PARENT

If all the duties and responsibilities of being a parent were written up in one big job description for people to consider before having kids, the world would have a lot fewer people in it. It's an all-encompassing role that requires outrageous amounts of hard work, self-sacrifice, and personal growth. It's a job that covers more roles than anyone can imagine, from teacher to chef to disciplinarian to chauffeur to cheerleader to personal assistant. The most important task, however? Creating a loving, nurturing, and safe relationship with your child.

Perhaps the second most important role in parenting is keeping focus on the end goal: To rear kids so that they manage themselves in healthy ways when they are grown. Yes, the daily stuff matters, but parents tap into their greater wisdom when they take a long-term perspective on challenges and imperfections. This perspective will require learning and growing, compromise and leadership, self-regulation and compassion . . . all focused on the end goal.

How a Parent's Role Changes

When your child is an infant, parents are responsible for *everything*. Practically nothing happens unless you do it. Adjusting to this level of responsibility is part of what's so hard about having a newborn. After that, parents spend the rest of their lives unlearning most of those lessons. When a child is young, the parent's role is that of the leader who guides with thoughtful awareness of the child's unique needs and preferences. As your child ages and becomes a teenager, the parent's role becomes supporting the teen's autonomy. Sometimes it's helpful to remember that parenting teenagers requires you to let go a little bit every day. There's not a single moment when a switch flips and they are ready to take over.

Rather, this transition of power unfolds in a gradual, imperfect way.

You may have a child who was born wanting to be in charge of their lives, or one who has to have responsibility thrust upon them. Either way, the process of maturing will happen despite their preferences. The world will treat them differently as they age, and your job is to prepare them for that change. That transition is often both a thrilling and terrifying experience for kids.

How a Child's Role Changes

When kids are young, they are hardwired to want to be in alignment with their parents. Yes, individuals vary, but in general, children want to please their parents. A child's default position is more in line with their parents' views than that of a teenager. As your children age, your desire to shape them in line with your values or preferences will have to be curbed. Teenagers are less willing to go along in the areas in which they differ from their parents (whether in belief, practice, behavior, or value). Importantly, this is biologically driven, and a necessary part of growing up. Teenagers are supposed to be separating from their parents, figuring out who they are, what their values are, and how to be a healthy, functioning, independent person in the world. Parents are supposed to support this process, a task as easy and straightforward as herding cats on a roller coaster.

REAL-LIFE SCENARIO

Kayla is 13, and after a year of begging, her mom, Rhonda, bought her a dog. Fast forward a few months, and despite all of Kayla's promises, the daily work of caring for the dog has fallen to Rhonda. Sometimes Kayla will help when asked, but she never owns the responsibility.

It's Thursday late afternoon, and Rhonda walks into the living room and tells Kayla that the dog needs to be walked. There is immediate pushback: "Nooooooooo." Rhonda feels instantly frustrated and starts lecturing Kayla about how she *begged* for the dog; the dog *needs* to be walked to be healthy; Kayla *promised* to be responsible; and so on. Then Rhonda says that she will walk the dog, but that if Kayla isn't ready and waiting to go with her in five minutes, it will be a problem. Kayla gets more upset and says, "But I need to work on my project now."

This makes Rhonda even more frustrated, because Kayla had told her earlier that she had finished all of her schoolwork so she could have screen time. They go back and forth a few more times, now arguing about work and honesty. Kayla gets so mad that she stomps off to her room, yelling complaints and excuses behind her as she goes and slamming her bedroom door.

The door slamming pushes Rhonda over the edge. She follows Kayla back to her room, barely holding herself together:

Rhonda: "Look at me! (Kayla doesn't turn around.) Do NOT slam the door! Look. At. Me."

Kayla: "You said not to look at you."

Rhonda: "No, I said look at me, so I can say this to you."

Kayla: "You said not to look at you."

Rhonda: "I said look at me."

Kayla: "You said not to look at you."

Rhonda: "ARGH!"

Rhonda's ready to explode but grips the air with her hands in frustration and then walks out, so she doesn't do more damage.

This true, and common, story is likely deeply relatable to parents of teenagers: Promises broken, responsibilities avoided, lies told, voices raised, doors slammed, and parents enraged. How is it possible that your teenager—someone you would literally die for—can sometimes make you feel violently angry toward them?

QUIZ: What Is Your Parenting Style?

1. Obedience is important to me as a parent—I expect to have control over my teenager.

    1. Practically Never
    2. Rarely
    3. Sometimes
    4. Usually
    5. Almost Always

2. I sometimes use physical means or shame/guilt to get control.

    1. Practically Never
    2. Rarely
    3. Sometimes
    4. Usually
    5. Almost Always

3. I regularly discover that my children have lied to me or have been sneaky behind my back in order to avoid limits or consequences I have set.

    1. Practically Never
    2. Rarely
    3. Sometimes
    4. Usually
    5. Almost Always

4. My teenager is primarily in charge of their academic life. I only help out when my assistance is requested.

    1. Practically Never
    2. Rarely
    3. Sometimes
    4. Usually
    5. Almost Always

5. I believe that teenagers should be given the opportunity to make mistakes, even ones that will impact other important areas of life.

   1. Practically Never
   2. Rarely
   3. Sometimes
   4. Usually
   5. Almost Always

6. Everyone in our house participates in chores, either on a schedule or by regularly pitching in when asked.

   1. Practically Never
   2. Rarely
   3. Sometimes
   4. Usually
   5. Almost Always

Please turn the page for scoring.

(continued)

Scoring: Questions 1–3

High scores are 10 and above. Low scores are five and below. The higher your score in this category, the more likely you are to want to have control over your teenager. Parents who want a high degree of control over their teenagers often have more conflictual relationships with their teens and lower satisfaction with their parenting life.

On the flip side, parents who have a tendency toward control also offer structure and consistency, both of which are positive elements of a healthy environment for growing young people. You may need to look for ways to keep the effective and positive structures, while simultaneously relaxing other areas. Try to increase (even if just by 20 percent) how often you allow your child to make mistakes and do things "their way," even when their way is unwise or even mildly unhealthy. If you score low, you are likely choosing relationship and good communication over control the majority of the time.

Scoring: Questions 4–6

High scores are 10 and above. Low scores are five and below. The higher your score in this category, the more likely it is that you offer your child age-appropriate independence. This is great. If your score is low, you may find that you can grow by allowing your child to hold power, even in the face of potentially negative consequences. It's hard to do, but effective parenting for teens requires that we let go of them a little bit every day. Flip back a page and reread the section on how our role changes as our kids age.

THE STRUGGLE OF PARENTING TEENS

Wading in the water at the beach with my family recently, I noticed that the sand under my feet was particularly unstable. The shifting sand made me keep moving, didn't feel solid, and was tiring to walk on. Teenage development is a lot like that sand for both parent and child. Your teenager's needs and preferences, moods, and growth often feel like shifting sand under your feet. It's hard to feel that you're on solid ground.

Parents often find that their teenagers are less cooperative, more reactive, and harder to influence than they used to be. Changing hormones and the developing teenage brain produce impulsivity, big feelings, and power struggles. The teenager's developmental need to explore their identity often means they want to go their own way, but they may not have the maturity or experience to make good choices. Parents often see their teens "trying on" new behaviors or attitudes that seem worrisome or dangerous. All of these changes leave parents feeling stressed, frustrated, and fearful. You want your child to grow up happy and healthy, and sometimes teenagers don't look as if they are going to turn out that way.

Independence

Despite the fact that transitioning from dependence to independence is a necessary and natural part of growing up, it isn't a smooth process for either parents or teenagers. Teenagers deeply want to feel their parents' trust and want to be allowed to try things on their own, to live parts of their lives without supervision, and to make decisions for themselves. They want to feel as if they are their own boss, at least *some* of the time. Unfortunately, parents don't always agree that teens are ready for the independence they seek. This happens sometimes because of the teenager's past performance, because of environmental risks, or because parents have a hard time letting go. Whatever the reason, the gap between how much independence your teen wants and how much you feel ready to give them can be a source of conflict.

Identity Formation

Another common underlying source of conflict between parents and teens is the hardwired drive to explore identity. Teenagers work to figure out how they are similar or different from parents, siblings, or peers. It's provocative and painful sometimes to be on the receiving end of a teenager's searching for identity, because it may involve rejecting, defying, or even belittling their parents. It is a process of experimentation, mistakes, and pivots. The 4th grader who was devoted to dance may want to quit her troupe as a teenager. The 7th grader who enthusiastically planned on a future career being a builder just like their dad may end up taking a totally different route in high school. Parents who question or resist these changes may encounter emotional responses from their teen. (Although even parents who simply note that the sky is blue may also experience emotional responses!)

Sexuality

Human biology dictates that the years between eight and 17 are a period of sexual maturation. Children's brains and bodies change and grow, including the development of external sex characteristics and an interest in romantic relationships. While most parents do want a healthy romantic partnership for their children *someday*, middle school and high school relationships can trigger significant anxiety for parents. It's hard to watch your kids practice and experiment with something so important. Parents may also have understandable fears about the outsized consequences that sexual experimentation can bring. Furthermore, many parents inherited a legacy of discomfort and silence when it comes to sexual education; while you may want to give your children more information than you had yourself, figuring out what they should know and when is daunting. The earlier you start talking with your child about sex, however, and the better your communication is in general, the easier it will be to talk about sex-related topics. It may be scary, but you'll be glad you did it.

THE CHALLENGE OF A DIGITAL WORLD

Parenting in the Information Age comes with unique challenges. The digital world provides culture and influences that parents can't control and sometimes don't even know about. Developing teens crave rich, engaging experiences that in turn shape their beliefs, values, and behavior. Online experiences may provide this, but often in ways that don't match a parent's values. Furthermore, if the parent doesn't even know what's happening, there isn't much they can do to provide counterbalancing influences.

Not all screen experiences are created equal. There are online experiences available that offer growth. There are also negative, unhealthy, or even dangerous experiences available online. Research has shown that overusing violent video games is associated with increased aggression, for instance. Other research has shown a correlation between increasing use of social media and frequency of depressive symptoms, especially for girls. Social media can painfully reveal to teens that they are being left out and make them feel that they are the only ones who aren't having fabulous experiences, even if you remind them that much of what they see is staged. Parents can't keep their kids from the digital world forever, and in fact it isn't healthy to try, but figuring out how to protect, moderate, teach, and role-model healthy use is a universal challenge.

The Pressure to Grow Up

Your teen's daily connection to the digital world can be a force for good and evil. Your teenager will be pushed to grow up, spend more, dress a certain way, and believe certain things as a result of their online practices. Yes, the trending pair of shoes is going to be more important to your teen than you might like. And yes, the Instagram influencers that your teen follows may not always promote things that are in alignment with your family's longstanding values. Nevertheless, your teenager might also start to read news articles about current events, or they may develop a passionate stance about a current social justice issue. Parents are left wondering how to minimize the negative influences without losing the positives.

A Balanced Approach

Parents have to find a place of balance by: providing boundaries around the unhealthiest content and practices; offering support for learning how to manage the addictive quality of screens; teaching critical thinking skills for consuming media; and role-modeling healthy screen practices. Remember, in a few years, your teenager is probably not going to live in your house anymore, and won't have anyone fussing at them to turn off their phone and go to bed. It will be their own job to value sleep and self-care, and their own challenge to unplug themselves from their devices. To get them ready for that independence, start with your own good role-modeling, and look for opportunities to teach skills for critical thinking and self-management. Those lessons will serve them much better in the long run than a highly controlled environment.

WHAT TEENS WANT

Teens want to be heard, included, and sometimes guided.

Teenagers Want to Be Heard

As teenagers leave childhood, they appreciate when their opinions are given weight. Teens want to have experiences in which their voices matter, where they are viewed as capable. Sometimes this shows up in small ways like picking a restaurant, or boycotting a company with unfair labor practices. Other times, it shows up in big ways like being an important part of a big family decision or successfully advocating for permission to drop out of a program of study they no longer find rewarding. Teens want to feel effective in creating change in the world they can see around them, especially in areas where that world affects them.

Teenagers Want and Need Inclusivity

Of course, teenagers want to be included by their peers, but they also want to be surrounded by a community that desires and expects good things for and from them. They crave a community, whether it be a school, neighborhood, team, or extended family that looks positively on them and their peers. Teens are naturally hyper aware of right and wrong and can thrive when surrounded by a just and supportive community. They want to be allowed to be themselves within their community, and they want that inclusivity to welcome others.

Developmentally, the teen years see a growth in the skill of perspective-taking. Teenagers are more capable, more skilled, and more likely to regularly see things from others' perspectives than kids are. This is certainly related to the teenage sensitivity to fairness and inclusion. In pursuit of a more just community and world, many teenagers find purpose and meaning in working to combat systemic injustice. Whether participating in a Black Lives Matter march, getting involved in a church youth group, or forming a band, teens gain self-expression and belonging in their efforts. When parents support them in their efforts, connection increases.

Still, our society supports some identities above others. Some teenagers may not feel or *be* safe due to their racial identity, citizenship status, sexual preference, gender expression, disability, or other authentic identity. Discrimination affects development and is traumatic. When a teen has an identity that causes them to experience discrimination, the presence or lack of their parent's support is fundamentally life-altering. As parents, you can, and should, support your teen as they navigate their authentic identity. Whether your teen needs emotional or practical support, for their own experiences or because they are standing up for others, the importance of a parent's support cannot be overstated.

Teenagers Want You to Guide Them . . . Sometimes

Part of normal teenage development is seeking distance from parents in emotional, physical, and supervisory ways. Parents have wisdom to share, a deep desire to help their teens avoid pitfalls, and teenage brains absolutely need adult support from time to time. However, parental guidance is not always welcome. Yes, teens want you available to them when *they* want you to be, but when parents think about guiding their teens, parents often imagine themselves in a more leading role than the one that usually works. In my practice, I often advise parents to ask their teenager's permission before giving advice, guidance, or sometimes even opinions. Experiment with this for yourself. Say: "I have an idea about something that might help with ___; would you like to hear it?" If they want your opinion, they will say yes. If they say no, you've saved both of you from an unwanted lecture. Your relationship will be the better for having asked first.

This is not to say, however, that teenagers don't need you to have their backs. As independent as teenagers may sometimes be, development isn't a straight line. Teenagers need and want to feel that you are still there for them. They need to know that someone's in their corner, that if they need backup, you are ready and willing. Teenagers also want the emotional support inherent in knowing that you believe, in general anyway, that when they take risks and try out new endeavors, they are making reasonable choices and are capable of getting something good from the process.

Great communication begins with connection.

OPRAH WINFREY

CHAPTER 2

FUNDAMENTAL COMMUNICATION SKILLS

When parents ask me for help talking to their teenager, I wish for a single concept that would make all the difference for them. But humans are complicated, and effective communication between parents and teenagers requires attention to many different moving parts. This chapter provides an overview of five essential communication skills for parents: active listening, nonverbal communication, authentic communication, emotional regulation, and emotional boundaries. The chapter also includes a real-life scenario about body piercing, and will cover the benefits of great family communication, and the complications of communication in the digital age.

REAL-LIFE SCENARIO

Mia is 16 and wants to get her nose pierced. The first time it comes up, it doesn't go well. Everyone is sitting at the table, and Mia's little brother slyly turns to her out of the blue and says, "Were you talking to your friend Shelli earlier? Why did you agree with her that you would both go get your noses pierced this weekend?" He, of course, only says this to get her in trouble with their parents, and it definitely works. Both parents react, with her mom, Erika, half yelling, "What!?" and her dad, Mike, booming, "That had better not be true." Neither parent is able to calm down and think clearly enough to have a useful conversation about it. It is a tense dinner, and Mia, furious with everyone, especially her brother, leaves after just a few minutes of picking at her food.

Erika and Mike talk privately about the scene later that night. They both feel strongly that nose piercing isn't something they are willing to permit at her age, but they also both feel strongly that the conversation about it had not gone well. They make a plan to revisit it, with just Mia, the next day.

Mia's parents begin with an apology. It isn't hard to imagine how crummy the experience must have been for her—being tattled on, having something she was excited about become a negative, and having both parents yelling at her at the same time. Erika and Mike acknowledge this, saying, "Look, we want to start out by apologizing to you. Dinner last night was stressful for everyone. We didn't handle ourselves well, and know that must have felt terrible for you. Nobody likes getting yelled at, and we're sorry."

This softens the feel of the room, which Erika can tell by the way Mia relaxes into her chair after they apologize. Plus, she makes eye contact with them for the first time since they knocked on her bedroom door. Her parents wait a minute, giving a little space for the apology to sink in, take a deep breath, and then say, "So can we rewind a little? Um, we hear you're thinking about a nose piercing. Would you tell us a little bit about that?"

Mia feels safe enough now to talk about the piercing. She tells them how her best friend's girlfriend got her nose pierced, and how it seems like a cool thing that she wants too. Mike asks some calm questions about what kind of jewelry she has in mind, where she thinks she might get it done, what it will cost, and what the piercing studio's policy is about minors. It becomes clear that the idea is more fantasy than plan.

Mia's parents keep the pace of the conversation slow and the tone relaxed. Erika asks Mia, "I'm sure you probably already have an idea of how we feel, given last night's ruckus,

(continued)

but can I tell you an opinion I have about piercings?" Mia rolls her eyes but doesn't actually look that annoyed by the question, and says, "Go ahead." Erika says, "I think it's a really big decision. When I was in college and my soccer team won the championship, we all agreed to get matching tattoos. But then we didn't agree on the design. We talked about options for a few weeks but pretty soon it just kind of stopped being a thing. Looking back on it now, I'm glad I didn't do it. Anyway, I know piercings and tattoos aren't the same thing, but my point is just that sometimes it's good to take it slow with big decisions."

Mia takes this in and, although she rolls her eyes again ever so slightly, says, "Yeah, yeah, okay, I get it. Big decision, take it slow; I got it." Mike and Erika ignore the eye rolling and recognize that this is as much of an agreement as they are going to get from her right now. Mike leans in and hugs her, saying, "We love you honey; thanks for letting us talk to you about this."

THE POWER OF EFFECTIVE COMMUNICATION

It's remarkable how many problems can be solved with thoughtful, calm discussion. But life with teenagers doesn't always make calm, thoughtful discussion easy. Some teenagers, like Mia in the scenario, will respond really well, and relatively easily, to their parent's efforts at active listening. A quiet and focused parent, undistracted, with welcoming nonverbal language and occasional clarifying questions can go a long way toward pulling more information and interaction out of a teenager. Some parents find that their own discomfort around a particular topic may be the cause of their communication difficulties, and figuring out how to speak authentically brings greater connection. Finally, fine-tuning the timing of communication, and being aware of and responsive to your teenager's emotional state is another significant step toward improved connection and communication. Having a variety of tools and strategies for removing barriers and improving communication takes time, but the lifelong benefits are immeasurable.

Active Listening

Active listening, explored in chapter 3, recognizes the powerful impact of treating communication as a two-way process. Whether you have a message you want to deliver, or you are responding to your child's message, your awareness of, and focus on, what the other person is saying, feeling, and experiencing in the moment is the "make it or break it" of effective communication. Active listening also empowers parents to recognize that what their child is saying with words may not reflect the entire larger meaning their child wants heard. Sometimes we have to "listen" beyond words in order to hear the truer meaning.

Authentic Communication

If you were raised in a home in which family secrets were everywhere, or in which your wants or needs couldn't be spoken aloud, you are likely to find authenticity in parenting to be both difficult and powerfully freeing. The truth *can* set you free. Authentic communication, the subject of chapter 4, can mean simply being able to recognize and speak your feelings, wants, wishes, dislikes, and boundaries. It can mean speaking your truth and *holding* your boundaries. It can mean speaking plainly, naming things, and not avoiding tough conversations. Authenticity in parenting can also mean allowing children to have an age-appropriate dose of reality. There is great power in being able to speak honestly and directly about what is in the world. We can—and should—be real about feelings and experiences. We can connect much more deeply with teens when we are real with them.

Nonverbal Communication

When there is an inconsistency between the message someone sends with their words and the message they send with their body, the nonverbal communication dominates. Nonverbal communication is powerful, quick, and not always explicitly taught or understood. Chapter 5 will detail the elements of nonverbal communication, including body position, facial expression, hand movements, tone of voice, and posture.

Emotional Regulation

Thanks to advances in brain imaging technology, we can now see which parts of our brain are activated while it is doing particular tasks. When experiencing high levels of emotional upset, parts of the brain shut down. Unfortunately, the parts of the brain that turn off when we are upset are vital to staying calm, resolving conflict, and communicating effectively.

Specifically, the upset brain loses skills like impulse control, organization and planning, empathy, morality, and seeing the "big picture." In other words, brains don't work properly when someone is really upset. Understanding this one concept discussed in chapter 6 and tweaking your actions and timing in difficult teenager moments, can practically add years to your life. Imagine the power in knowing when your teenager's brain is able to listen and think properly versus when anything you say is likely to just make the situation worse.

Emotional Boundaries

An emotional boundary, the focus of chapter 7, is a psychological delineation between the emotional experiences of two people. The boundary is where one person's feelings stop and the other person's feelings start. To say it another way, an emotional boundary is the border of our separateness. The feelings you have may be important to me, but they are not my feelings. Healthy emotional boundaries between parents and teens mean that the parents don't take the teen's emotions on as their own. Taking on your teen's emotions as your own can lead to parental overinvolvement and control.

Healthy emotional boundaries facilitate effective communication. Teenagers often react poorly to parents who are overly involved, and will start to push back against those boundary crossings in the only way they know how: shutting the parent out or slowing or stopping communication. Conversely, when teenagers know that their parents will practice good boundaries, and will allow the teenager to express feelings without those feelings triggering the parent to react in fear or judgment, for example, teens are far more likely to open up to their parents about sensitive topics.

THE BENEFITS OF EFFECTIVE COMMUNICATION

Effective communication allows us to get our needs met, feelings recognized, expectations fulfilled, misunderstandings cleared up, and problems repaired. It is a foundation for all relationships, and relationships are the foundation for all other growth. A teenager's lifelong well-being grows from their early primary relationships. Likewise, the parent–teen relationship deeply affects the parents' well-being. When the relationship is good, everyone benefits. When the relationship is in conflict, everyone suffers. Better communication makes better relationships, and better relationships mean better mental and physical health.

Teens are developmentally supposed to be challenging, experimenting, and exploring. Being able to communicate as they do so allows them to challenge, experiment, and explore in a "safe-enough" zone, and it helps parents feel "safe enough" to let them do it. When good communication isn't present, parents feel vulnerable and scared about their teenager's exploration. Teenagers who are cut off from their parents often fare much worse for not having the tether to safety and health that a parent provides.

Better Relationships and Attunement

Healthy, happy relationships require space for emotions. When someone has a complaint, can they voice it? Can two people talk through disagreements? Feeling able to express yourself, feeling safe to have your feelings, feeling as if someone understands you even when you are upset or mad: these are core parts of a healthy relationship. Teenagers, as they work to develop their identity, want to be able to express themselves and be heard. When a parent and child have the ability to communicate about big things, delicate things, important things, painful things, it reflects on the overall relationship in significant and positive ways. It is relationship-building to talk about important stuff, and when parents do it well, each conversation lays down another foundational layer in the relationship.

Effective communication in parenting requires an accurate recognition of your teenager's current emotional state (and your emotional state, too, actually). What parent hasn't had the experience of asking a simple question and being met with a rude response? Teens are less likely to respond in rude or sassy ways when they feel understood. Being aware of and responsive to your teenager's emotional state is a powerful way to maximize the effectiveness of any communication. This is called attunement.

We can further define attunement as an almost unconscious awareness that a parent or caregiver has about how an experience, dynamic, or interaction is going to feel for the child. For example, an attuned caregiver knows that it's going to rub the teenager the wrong way to ask if she took out the trash, right after she just stubbed her toe. Or, the parent knows that today might not be the best day to bring up the fact that a cousin just got a college scholarship offer from his first-choice school, when their son just got a rejection letter from his. Having an attuned parent makes children feel emotionally safe, and effective communication is key to developing attunement in relationships.

Less Conflict and Fewer Misunderstandings

Many conflicts have their origins in misunderstandings. For example, one person says "short trip" and another assumes that's 10 minutes, but it turns out to be 45. The mismatched expectations leave one person feeling resentful and disappointed and the other feeling unfairly judged. When people can be direct and clear about their needs, preferences, and expectations, they can often sidestep conflict. Furthermore, letting your teenager see you working to understand them is good for the relationship. It shows your teenager that, even though there may be a gap between what the two of you think, gaining understanding with them is a priority for you. That's a powerful message to send.

Kids who feel that communication is effective, safe, and embraced by their parents are more likely to come to their parents when they need information or help. This is exactly what parents want, because as parents, we are more likely to offer wise and accurate guidance and reasonable, healthy support than other possible sources like friends or the internet.

The Teen's Mental and Physical Health

The research about how communication and the parenting relationship shapes children and teenagers is clear: Better communication equals better relationships, and better relationships produce improved mental and physical health. Conversely, poor relationships are associated with worse outcomes. The science demonstrates it, and it feels intuitively true. For example, research has shown that teenagers who have poor relationships with their parents are more likely to be diagnosed with depression as teens. Trust issues between mother and teens in the 6th grade lead to higher levels of depression by 12th grade. Effective communication about sex between parents and teens results in teens delaying sex and having safer sex. Overall, positive family relationships are associated with lower rates of depression all the way through midlife.

The Parent's Mental and Physical Health

And it's not just the teenagers benefitting from the positive communication. Research reveals that the parent–teen relationship shapes *parental* mental and physical health as well. In fact, parental well-being is generally lower during adolescence than in infancy and early childhood. Parents, and in particular mothers, report more stress and less meaning in their lives during their kids' adolescence. Imagine then, the pivotal role that good communication can play in the parent's overall mental health and well-being. In a stage in which parental happiness is already taxed, being able to make the parent–child relationship stronger through effective communication means more connection and more joy. And certainly, less stress resulting from better communication will benefit the parents physically, because there is universal agreement that stress causes physical toll on all of the body's systems, including, for example, the cardiovascular and gastrointestinal systems.

EFFECTIVE COMMUNICATION IN A DIGITAL WORLD

Let's turn our focus to the unique challenges that digital communication brings. Although it can be tempting to rail against the "evils" lurking in our children's devices, it will be easier to connect with our teenagers if we start from a place of positive, if cautious, appreciation for technology. Thanks to their smartphones and other devices, teens today have access to information of any kind. From help with a specific geometry proof to learning how to sew a scrunchie to current events, they can, and do, learn voraciously online. Teenagers also get a lot of their social needs met via connecting with people online. Importantly, teenagers, particularly those who have difficulty with social connection or who are in marginalized communities, may find much-needed support online, in the forms of identity-based affinity groups.

The advantages of the online, technological world are worth the work required to help children learn and grow the skills they need to manage the challenges that accompany the digital world. Here is some guidance to help you maximize the good and minimize the bad.

Things to Know

◆ What does your teenager like to do online? Know what their favorite apps or social media platforms are, and have at least basic knowledge of how they work, so you can relate to them at least on a fundamental level.

◆ Stay current on screen-use recommendations and best practices. For example, it is recommended that personal digital devices be kept out of bedrooms at night. The American Academy of Pediatrics is a great resource for screen-time recommendations.

◆ Determine whether your teenager shares their passwords with their friends, and go over the pros and cons of that level of access. See more information in the resources section, page 135.

◆ Figure out the privacy practices/limitations of certain apps that track your teen's information and behavior.

Things to Do

- Reach out to your teen digitally from time to time. We have to connect with kids "where they are," and your teen is online. If your teenager is secretive with you about their online world, that can be a sign that your relationship has some elements of mistrust in it. You may find chapter 7 on boundaries, and the upcoming section about device privacy, to be particularly helpful.

- Have, communicate, and maintain reasonable, healthy policies about screen use. Start with their first device, because younger kids, and kids who are new to a technology, are more likely to accept and follow use policies.

- Model the behaviors you want your teen to emulate. The parent who brings their phone to the dinner table can't expect their teenager to do differently.

- Talk with your teenager about healthy behavior online such as identity, personal security, sharing personal information or revealing photos, and interfacing with strangers. Discuss how to set boundaries with a device and with the ways that people can reach you through it; help teens learn how *not* to be always reachable.

- Effective communication about screen use and behavior doesn't happen in one big conversation. Look for teachable, talkable moments over a span of years. For example, the valuable reminder that "things posted online are generally there forever" is easily revisited when there's a story in the news of someone experiencing consequences for old posts or pictures.

Device Privacy

Device privacy means many things, but most importantly it refers to whether you as a parent have reserved the right to look through your child's device at any time. This is a practice that many parents feel is important when their kids get their first device. They believe that the possibility of "supervision anytime" helps kids to form good habits about online behavior. As children age and move into the teen years, a lack of device privacy becomes increasingly offensive to teens. When your teenager is younger, discuss your policy related to device privacy openly. It's much better to have a conflict over the fact that she knows you look at her texts sometimes than for her to discover belatedly that you have been "spying" on her. When your teenager is older, it's recommended that parents offer device privacy, because not allowing a teenager to have privacy sends a powerful message of mistrust.

One of the most essential ways of saying "I love you" is being a receptive listener.

FRED ROGERS

CHAPTER 3

KEY SKILL: ACTIVE LISTENING

In our primary relationships, listening is love, and building better skills in listening to our teenagers has great value. This chapter reviews the elements of active listening, and offers concrete advice on putting the skills into practice. This chapter includes real-life scenarios about talking with a teen in an accepting way about sexuality, specifically bisexuality, and about managing disappointment. Because the process of parenting teens often triggers judgment on the part of the parents, the chapter closes with an exercise that will help you move from judgment to compassion.

REAL-LIFE SCENARIO

Maria and David's daughter Lucia came out to them as bi a while back, but she hasn't said much of anything about romantic relationships ever since. This morning Maria happens to see a message flash up on Lucia's lock screen that make it seem as if Lucia's *friend* Jeannine might actually be her *girlfriend* Jeannine, something Lucia hasn't mentioned.

Maria and David agree that they want to take every opportunity to demonstrate their acceptance and support of Lucia's sexuality. They also want to find a way to open the lines of communication about sexuality and romantic relationships, at least insofar as Lucia is comfortable. That evening, they get an opportunity: Lucia walks in while Maria and David are prepping dinner. David asks: "How was your day?" Lucia sighs and starts talking: "Jeannine is being weird. I don't think we're going to that movie this weekend after all."

Maria turns around to face Lucia and asks, "Jeannine's being weird about your plans?"

"Yeah, like, first she wanted to go with just me, but then she said she had invited Ellis and Kai to come, too. I'm starting to think that she doesn't want to hang out alone with me. Is she planning to break up with me and doesn't think she can act normal alone? I don't know what's going on."

Maria and David know Ellis well and think she isn't a great influence, but recognize that this isn't the moment to say anything about that. Instead, David says, "Oh, man, two extra people on what maybe was supposed to be a date? That IS weird . . ."

Lucia nods her head and doesn't say much else. After a couple beats, Maria says, "Yeah, I'd feel weird, too. And hurt, honestly."

Lucia looks at her mom and nods again. "Yeah, if she's going to break up with me, I wish she'd just get it over with, instead of dragging it out and inviting people along to our movie."

Maria, David, and Lucia keep talking for another minute or two, with her parents mostly just affirming her perspective and offering support. They don't mention their concerns about the other teenager, and they don't complain about the fact that Lucia hadn't told them she was dating Jeannine. Privately, later, Lucia's parents relive the talk. It felt like a great connection point, one in which they were able to be supportive, and Lucia seemed comfortable opening up. Parenting win.

WHAT IS ACTIVE LISTENING?

Busy parents are often masters of multitasking. You can probably start dinner while also unloading the dishwasher, answering a text, and listening to your kid tell a story about school. Modern life requires this, and sometimes it's the only way to get all the things done. But there is a different kind of listening that parents can and should utilize when having an important conversation with their teenager.

Active listening involves giving the speaker all of your attention (no multitasking), paying attention to explicit and implicit cues, paying attention to sensory cues and underlying meaning, suspending judgment and prioritizing understanding, and actively signaling with your own body, facial expressions, eye contact, and vocalizations that you are focused, understanding, and present. Active listening is work. It's also a powerful way to make the speaker feel important, valued, and understood. Here, we break down some of the components of active listening.

Prioritizing the Speaker

The first component of active listening is focusing on the speaker and their message, and deprioritizing everything else. Put down the phone, the spatula, and the paperwork. Give your teen your full attention, and work hard to ignore everything else. It isn't always possible, though, so if you can't, say so and ask for a raincheck. That might sound like, "Sweetheart, I really want to hear your story, but what I'm working on is due in 30 minutes. I've got to get this finished, but as soon as I'm done, I'd love to talk to you. Can I come find you in a little bit?"

Demonstrate Listening

Parents often find that they have to stop their body's movement in order to focus fully. This actually serves two goals because a shift in your body position—sitting down, for example—not only helps with focus, but is a nonverbal cue that says you are relaxed and attentive. Maria, in the real-life scenario on page 34, stopped preparing dinner and turned her body to face Lucia, for example. Chapter 5 will go into body language in much more depth. For now, to demonstrate listening, have a neutral, mildly positive, or compassionate facial expression, lean in slightly, uncross your arms, nod occasionally, and keep your attention on what your teenager is saying.

Withholding Judgment

Often, your thoughts may be critical, either of your teenager and what they did, of others, or perhaps of yourself. Sometimes that voice wants you to tell your child what they should do to solve the problem. This voice is unhelpful to the process of active listening. Once the critic in your head starts ranting, it's no longer possible to be fully focused on, and present with, your teenager. This is especially true when parents are feeling fear about their child's future or shame about their own mistakes in parenting. Work to connect with the calm, wise voice inside your head, the one that helps you attain peace and see the bigger picture. Then, take a deep breath and refocus on what your child is saying. Don't give voice to the criticism or advice.

Sometimes our loved ones just need a place to vent. A teenager exclaiming, "My teacher is so unfair! I just wanted to kill him!" probably doesn't mean that murder is imminent. Even if they are threatening big actions, like "I'm going to quit the team!" or "I'm never going back to school!" it's okay to just suspend reality for a moment. Be present for the underlying emotion (resentment, frustration, hopelessness, etc.); connect with your children about the pain first, and withhold judgment, reaction, or advice about the particular behavior, words, or threats. Indeed, being present without judgment or advice is often the single most effective way to help someone calm down from big feelings.

Reflecting

As you continue to stay focused and present, without allowing your own thoughts and judgments to distract you from what your teenager is saying, you can begin to use a few carefully selected verbal techniques. Start with reflecting what your teenager is saying. This is where you simply repeat back what you heard, often using almost the exact same phrasing. It can take a bit of practice to be able to parrot someone in a way that feels supportive and not patronizing or mocking. It's helpful to put a bit of emotion into the statement, mirroring a small percentage of the emotion your teenager was expressing earlier. This might sound like "Oh man, your teacher is so *unfair*. It's making you *so* mad, you feel murderous!" Or, "Yikes! That was such a big deal you don't *ever* want to go back there again." Notice that your words in this step do not include advice, guidance, or opinion; only reflection. This is because your goal here is for your teenager to feel that you are "meeting them where they are," which is very different from telling them what to do.

Clarifying

As this conversation continues to unfold, you might ask your teenager a question or two. You may just ask questions to make sure you heard the message accurately, in case the emotions took over and your teen didn't make complete sense. This might sound like "So, the band director said you can't try out for jazz band because you didn't participate in regionals?" Or, "So you said you didn't want to go and then she called you—a *what*?!"

Sometimes, when stories don't fully make sense to a parent, clarification can help get to the essence of the upset: "Okay, this whole story feels bad, but is there a part that's *especially* upsetting to you? Would you tell me that part again?" Clarifying can also serve as a de-escalation technique, because the experience of being really heard is soothing.

It's important to be aware of and manage your own feelings here, so your clarifying questions don't sound like, "Why didn't you handle that better?" Early in my career, a mentor told me that the only answer to the question of "Why did you do that?" is some variation of "Because I'm a bad person." I have found this to be especially true between parents and teenagers. Be careful with "why" questions; they are often just lightly disguised judgments.

Summarizing and Validating

The final active listening techniques are summarizing what you heard the other person say and validating what they've said. You've kept their message (both explicit and implicit) in mind, and are able to convey it back to them in a clear way. You demonstrate here that you have been listening, that they have been heard, and that their message has been accurately delivered and received. You do *not* necessarily say that you agree or that you believe them.

Additionally, in the style of couple's counseling called Imago, developed by Dr. Harville Hendrix and Dr. Helen LaKelly Hunt, therapists teach a step-by-step dialogue that uses validation after summarizing. Validation does not imply agreement, but it does take summarizing one step further, providing an affirmation of sorts, and can be particularly effective in communication between parents and teens. This validation usually includes a statement indicating that the teen makes sense, with a brief explanation of how their feelings or perspective makes sense.

Our teens need to know that we think they are reasonable and relatable and that their upsets make sense to us, given what we know about them. Parents can convey that validation—without expressing agreement or assent—by simply saying, "That makes sense to me." (Or, *you* make sense to me.) "It makes sense to me that you would feel that way/would be upset about that/etc." "I'd be upset about that, too, if I were in your shoes."

PUTTING IT INTO ACTION

When my children were young toddlers, I learned the hard way that I'm not a great parent at 2 a.m. If I think I'm supposed to be doing something else, sleeping for example, I find it hard to be present, compassionate, and patient. When we aren't at our best, we don't parent our best. But since two-year-olds don't really care about our parenting insights, I had to find concrete ways to support myself to be the best parent I could in the situation. Active listening is similar: Much of the advice about active listening is probably familiar to you. But the magic doesn't start until we find actual ways to insert it into our daily lives: to make it our reality. The following three concrete strategies can help you put active listening into action: limiting distractions, listening to what's being said (and not what you want to say), and being okay with silence.

Limit Distractions

I think it's fair to say that I have pretty good listening skills (I am a therapist, after all). So does that mean I always listen really well to my children? Definitely not. I'm no different from you in that distraction limits my presence and engagement, and my kids can tell the difference: "Mom. Mom! Are you listening to me?" My attempts to juggle 10 things at once have to be curbed, and sometimes I have to have little talks with myself about what my priorities really are.

This is part of why teenagers tend to open up in the car; it's a quiet time when parents are, ironically, more available than usual. But as parents, we have to recognize that undistracted conversations are important, and we have to carve out space for them. We have to say no to the other distractions in the moment. Consider setting aside a few minutes every day to be alone with and focused on your teenager, or turn off the device you're working on (if you can) when your teen starts talking to you, at least once a day. Give connection time with your teenager precedence when you can, and remember that you may have to be available for some time before your teen will take advantage of such moments.

There will be times when your teen can't be the priority, and that's okay. Just acknowledge that and be sure to circle back as soon as they can be the priority. Crises can't be scheduled, but the layers of regular daily connection can. A dozen little conversations about the finicky theater teacher's latest offenses can add up for a teenager who feels as if he isn't alone in dealing with the experience.

Pay Attention to What's Being Said, Not to What You Want to Say

Active listening gets a whole chapter in this book because communication is rarely good when it's a one-way street. Consider author Stephen Covey's famous quote: "Most people do not listen with the intent to understand; they listen with the intent to reply." Think about how it felt the last time you had a conversation like that, one in which the other person wasn't listening to you at all. Those conversations are unsatisfying at best, and are sometimes painful. If a topic is important to you, if the relationship is important to you, then the other person's true listening is also important to you.

Our kids need this kind of listening from us, and when we are listening "to reply" they aren't getting what they need. The first step is slowing down our own internal reply process. Notice when your internal voice has become louder than the other person's actual voice. Are you feeling worried that you have to convince your teenager to come around to your perspective?

If you find that you are listening in order to reply, it may be that you are trying to control your teenager through ideological power struggling. Stop. It doesn't work. Arguing with teenagers rarely produces a good outcome. Rather, the strength of a person's beliefs often *increases* when they have to defend themselves. (Conversely, when someone feels heard and understood, they are often more likely to compromise.)

So, take a deep breath, and relax the muscles in your body. Tell yourself that it's okay for the two of you to have different opinions or perspectives. Remind yourself that parents only have control over some things, and your teenager's thoughts aren't one of those things. Remind yourself that you love this teenager very much, and it's important to them to be heard and understood by their parent. Stop trying to reply, and instead refocus your energy on understanding their perspective as best you can.

Be Okay with Silence

Active listening thrives with silence. If you aren't listening in order to craft your retort, and the other person stops talking, there's going to be a pause. That pause has value. Silence allows us to feel and uncover emotions. Silence allows the speaker's words to "ring" longer, which amplifies the experience of being heard.

Our job isn't to prevent others from feeling their feelings, or to fix those feelings for them (see chapter 7), so there is no reason to rush through a silence. Give yourself permission to close your eyes briefly and take a deep breath. (Yes, you're going to get this advice from me several times in this book, but the repetition is purposeful.) Use that moment to reset, relax your muscles, slow your heartbeat. As our bodies calm, it gets easier to both feel connected and be aligned with the other person, even if your opinions are opposed.

On the other hand, if your teenager finds the silence goes on for too long and gives you the "Well, say something!" look, you can shake your head in acknowledgment and say, "Oh, sorry, I was just thinking about what you said," and then go ahead with your reply. In so many parts of parenting, your goal is to find the right "dose" for your child of any particular intervention, so give yourself permission to experiment a little.

Exercise: From Judgment to Compassion

When problems arise, it's generally unhelpful for parents to be judgmental toward their kids. Judgment is often a way we cope with, or defend against, feelings of fear or shame. Instead, work to *feel* and *communicate* the emotion of compassion. The word compassion comes from a Latin root meaning to "suffer with." Use this exercise to help you shift emotionally during those times when your child's emotions or behavior causes you uncomfortable feelings and judgmental reactions.

(continued)

Briefly describe the challenging situation and your child's response.

_____

_____

_____

_____

_____

_____

_____

_____

_____

_____

_____

_____

What is going on for my child emotionally? What do I think they are feeling deep down? (It helps to tell the story from their perspective.)

_____

_____

_____

_____

_____

_____

_____

_____

_____

_____

_____

Recall a time in your own life (ideally your teen years) when you felt those feelings or similar ones. The situation can be different; we're just looking for emotional connection. What was it like for you when you felt those feelings?

_____

_____

_____

_____

_____

_____

_____

_____

_____

_____

_____

Imagine your most supportive adult (from your teen years) at that time saying to you: "You know, it makes sense to me that you did that/felt that way. I know that experience must have been _____ (scary, overwhelming, embarrassing, desperate, etc.) for you." How might that have felt at the time? How would it have felt to get compassion and understanding from someone who cared about you?

_____

_____

_____

_____

_____

_____

_____

_____

_____

_____

_____

Now imagine how it might feel to your teenager to receive that sort of support from you today. Can you channel that? What makes sense about their underlying feeling? Write it down. Connect their action (however unwanted) to their feeling. Aim to connect compassionately with the feeling as you write.

_____

_____

_____

_____

_____

_____

_____

_____

_____

_____

_____

REAL-LIFE SCENARIO

Chris's son Leon had basketball tryouts this afternoon. Leon wants to be on the varsity team but was having an off day and didn't perform well, so wasn't picked. He's feeling upset, jealous, and angry and is complaining about the coach and the other team members. Chris feels triggered by Leon's venting, because sportsmanship is a very important value to Chris. He's just on the cusp of starting to lecture Leon, but catches himself and pauses to take a deep breath.

Chris remembers that Leon needs to be seen from a compassionate perspective, even when his behavior looks bad. Chris takes another deep breath, closes his eyes for a second, and starts trying to remember what it was like to be 14. He thinks:

> *If I were 14 again, with an immature brain, having worked hard and come up short in a very public way, I might not have what it takes to handle feelings of disappointment and embarrassment maturely,*

(continued)

either. I might throw a bit of a tantrum myself. I might say ugly things and blame others, all in an attempt to save face and protect myself from those overwhelming feelings of failure. I guess I'm impressed that he was able to hold it in until we got home. Sure, I want Leon to mature and do better, but I can understand and be compassionate about how he fell short today. I believe that Leon is someone who will grow and do better in the future. He needs me to be on his side today, not offering more criticism or judgment than he is already feeling.

Chris digs deep and refocuses on what Leon is saying, especially working to suspend his judgment. Chris gives him a little longer to vent and offers love and compassion. Leon eventually softens and calms down, and he eventually pulls out his phone to send a congratulatory text to his friend who did make the team.

Authenticity is the daily practice of letting go of who we think we're supposed to be and embracing who we are.

BRENÉ BROWN

CHAPTER 4

KEY SKILL: AUTHENTIC COMMUNICATION

Being authentic means allowing your deepest self to be reflected in your words and actions; it means being unguarded and vulnerable. Authenticity, though it can be scary, leads to deeper and better relationships, and authenticity in the parent–teen relationship is linked with lower rates of depression. Teenagers have a deep appreciation for when people are being real with them.

This chapter will cover what parents have to know and do to be authentic in their communication. This includes knowing yourself, knowing and accepting your child, and embracing your reality. The chapter includes advice about direct communication, telling the truth and avoiding family secrets, and the benefits of an "age-appropriate" dose of reality. This chapter also includes a real-life scenario about learning disabilities, and another about talking with a biracial child about how to behave during police encounters.

REAL-LIFE SCENARIO

Fadya and Asad are parents to 13-year-old Adam. Adam has a diagnosis of autism spectrum disorder and ADHD. His neuro divergencies contribute to challenges at school, and he has received special education services since 3rd grade. Adam and his parents have had dozens of conversations about school and what's hard about it, but Adam's parents have never talked to him about his diagnoses. They especially avoid talking about his autism diagnosis, and in fact, have never even said the word in front of him. Fadya has wanted to, but Asad is afraid that it will make Adam feel different or not good enough.

Not talking about Adam's diagnosis directly has started to get harder, because Adam has started asking questions. He came home from school today and asked: "Why do I have to go to Ms. Richard's class? She doesn't teach anything—she just talks to me about what the other teachers are doing. No other 7th graders go to her!"

Fadya feels defensive immediately. She notices that her heart begins to race, and her stomach feels tied in knots. She turns away from Adam before answering: "Well, that's not true, Adam! Lots of kids go see Ms. Richard."

He responds, "How do you know? Why do *I* have to see her? I don't want to go anymore."

Fadya isn't sure what she can say that truly answers Adam's question, without bringing up his diagnosis or his Individualized Education Plan (IEP). She attempts to make her voice light, and although she's still not facing Adam, she shrugs her shoulders and says, "She is a nice lady. She likes you and wants to help you with school!"

"But why do I have to go to her class?!"

Fadya feels trapped. She thinks fast, trying to come up with the right thing to say. Before she comes up with a reply, Adam groans in frustration and bemoans, "I hate school!"

Adam stomps off to his room, and Fadya is left feeling frustrated and trapped. She doesn't want to stray from the agreement she made with her husband, but she thinks Adam is directly asking for this information, and she feels badly keeping it from him. It feels like a lose-lose at this point. But now that they have kept it from him, she's afraid it's going to be a big deal when they do finally tell him: He's going to be angry with her for avoiding his questions. She's also afraid that it's going to make him feel worse about himself and hurt their relationship.

WHAT IS AUTHENTIC COMMUNICATION?

Being authentic is defined as being true to who you are, what you believe, and to your feelings and preferences. Authentic communication means you strive to let your outside self, your words, and your actions reflect the values you genuinely believe in and the messages you intend to deliver. Authentic communication requires a safe space, because it's hard to be authentic when you believe you will have to defend or protect yourself. Authentic communication includes being direct and clear, facing reality, and being a truth-teller. It requires knowing yourself, your child, and your reality.

Authenticity Requires Introspection and Knowing Yourself

Before you can be authentic, you have to be introspective, because knowing your truths requires self-awareness and self-examination. Therapy, journaling, or a mindfulness practice are some methods you might use to identify your inner feelings and beliefs. This work can feel vulnerable, scary, freeing, and empowering. Once you have an explicit understanding of your internal beliefs and preferences, authentic living includes words and actions that reflect and honor your inner truth.

Authenticity also requires an awareness of your inner emotional life. Humans feel emotions in their brains *and* bodies. Developing the ability to recognize how particular emotions feel in your body is an important skill for teens and adults. The embodied experience of an emotion, for example a knotted-up gut, can tell us something that our consciousness may have glossed over. We can't be authentic if we aren't tuned in to our deepest emotions. Authentic communication happens best when we make sure that our outer emotional expression—words and body language—matches our inner emotional experiences.

Teenagers Highly Value Authenticity

Teenagers want their parents to live according to well-reasoned beliefs, even though the teens may experiment with their own identities and are still figuring out their inner truths. The reason is that teens question authority, and they will trust you more if you, too, have questioned authority and come out on the other side with your own well-thought-out reasons for your actions and beliefs. The more deeply you know yourself and the more consistently you live a life based on your values, the more you can count on your teenager to do the same, even though they may spend a few years experimenting with other values. Parents are the best people to teach values to teens. Teenagers *do* want parents to share their important values with them, although they won't always show it. One way to share these values is through authentic communication.

Knowing Your Child

Parents-to-be have ideas about who their future kids will be and how they will parent them. These are often unrealistic ideas. Before I became a parent, I knew with certainty that I would *never* be the kind of mother who peeled apples for her child. You can guess how that turned out. This also shows up with personality trait differences, and it's especially evident in the teen years. You assumed your child would share your passions and your preferences, such as wanting to be active outdoors, or excelling in math. Sometimes parents have a hard time accepting that their child is different from them, and it can feel sad, disappointing, and worrisome. Sometimes this manifests itself in nagging and conflict. Parents can find themselves locked in self-conflict over their child's identity, preferences, productivity, or future goals, to name a few. In these types of situations, the relationship suffers, because parents aren't seeing their teenager for who they really are, and authentic communication will be difficult.

Even more challenging is when a parent's unmet expectations are about big stuff, such as when children have an exceptionality or diagnosed problem. Sometimes the parents' worries or disapproval (lack of acceptance) can hinder the teen in having the types of experiences, including failures, that provide opportunities for growth.

Parents are at their best when they see their child for who they really are and accept them for it. Sometimes this takes a professional to work through—a therapist or a parent coach, or perhaps a parenting support group. It's normal to have feelings of grief to process; the loss of the traits you had hoped for in your child is a real thing to mourn. It's worth the effort, though, because it can enable you to move on and accept the traits your child does have. Additionally, important outcomes rely on this true acceptance: Children can't be safe, happy, and healthy if they aren't seen and understood by their parent. Your relationship with your child requires your accurate understanding and acceptance.

Acknowledging Reality

Parenting doesn't happen in a vacuum, and the ways the outside world reaches into our lives aren't always welcome or healthy. It's hard to know when to be completely open and honest versus when to shield children. However, by the time your child is a teenager, it's generally time for them to be aware of the realities of the outside world. The key is to look for moments to gradually give your child age-appropriate doses of reality. For example, Fadya might have had success talking with Adam about his neurodiversity when he started receiving special education in 3rd grade. She might have explained neurodiversity and special education by saying something like, "Everyone's brains are different, and it's the school's job to teach all the different kinds of brains in the ways they learn best. Those tests you took helped your school understand that your brain will learn better in a classroom like Ms. Richard's."

One of the more painful types of authentic communication that parents struggle with is how to help their teen make sense of pain and suffering. If your teenager has something in their life that brings them discomfort, avoiding the topic isn't going to change the fact that the discomfort exists. Rather, it's likely to make the discomfort worse because your teen has to make sense of the problem *and* deal with it on their own. When, for example, teenagers have a loved one who has an addiction problem, when there has been a suicide, divorce, past mental health difficulties, or other truths sometimes considered "unmentionable," it doesn't serve teens to keep them out of the loop. Rather, authentic communication means that we work through our own feelings about those truths and find ways to talk about the truths in age-appropriate ways.

PUTTING IT INTO ACTION

Authentic communication is highly valuable to teenagers; they hold a special level of disdain for moments when parents aren't being genuine with them. Teens can often tell when their parent's inner and outer truths aren't in alignment. Practice authentic communication techniques with your teenager by communicating directly, clearly, and concisely; planning conversations ahead of time; telling the truth; presenting reality in doses as age-appropriate; and seeking support when needed.

Communicate Directly

Some families communicate directly, meaning they ask for what they want and expect a yes or no response. Other families aren't as direct and the communication more closely resembles hints and guesses. In addition to generational and familial trends, there are powerful cultural influences in how directly you deliver messages like requests, disagreement, or problems. Directness will vary between parents and cultures. Nonetheless, it is still important for all parents to keep in mind that some degree of directness is important in communicating with teens. When parents aren't direct, children can fill in the gaps with incorrect information. Worse, when children register that a topic can't be discussed openly, they believe that they can't ask questions or seek support when something goes wrong. This is a real obstacle to authentic communication. If the topic is important, parents should strive to be clear and direct with their children about it.

Communicate Clearly and Concisely

When you need to have an important conversation with your teenager, try to keep it short and sweet. For example, when coaching divorcing parents about how to tell their kids, I often advise them to prepare a two- to three-sentence introductory statement, then just listen after they've said those words. Take the example with Fadya and Adam. After discussing it with her husband and some advance planning about the conversation, she could come up with a few sentences of authentic, honest response to Adam's questions about why he has to see Ms. Richard. Before crafting her response, she needs to take into account the fact that he isn't asking for data but rather is expressing his embarrassment, frustration, and confusion. She could start with something like, "It sounds as if you're not loving the class, huh?" and then when she senses that he is ready, explain to him, very simply, his diagnoses, and then be prepared to sit calmly and let him express what he needs to express and answer his questions.

Effective communication with teenagers requires two-way conversation, one in which both parents and teens are sharing and listening. Is there more to say about an impending divorce than three sentences can convey? Of course, but that's the point: You want to start a conversation, not perform a monologue. Tuning in to how your words "land" and noticing the signals your child is already sending after a couple of sentences helps prevent conversations from turning into lectures. Parents should strive to keep their messages clear and concise. Don't push the limits of how much your teen can tolerate before listening shuts down.

Some Conversations Need Planning

Having worked with many parents as they consider how to have difficult conversations with their kids, I can assure you that preplanning is a key element to success. Big conversations benefit tremendously when parents think through what they want to say. If two parents are involved, talking about and agreeing on what will be said can prevent uncomfortable surprises later on. Likewise, thinking through when and where conversations will happen can also help. Imagine the impact of learning a piece of difficult news, or talking about a hard decision when you are supposed to be studying for a final tomorrow, or after a really bad day at school. Give all family members the benefit of a calm, private, and distraction-free time for important conversations.

Additionally, planning and preparation create additional opportunities for a parent to identify the emotions that might be embedded in a difficult conversation. One of the hardest things about some conversations is maintaining the ability to think clearly when feeling strong feelings. We can help ourselves avoid this pitfall by mentally rehearsing some parts of the conversation. Imagine how the conversation will unfold, and let yourself feel the feelings. This "dress rehearsal" can help you feel more emotionally present when you have the real conversation with your child.

Tell the Truth. Don't Have Family Secrets.

Family secrets rarely turn out well. While it may be tempting to do so, it is never a good idea to keep big secrets from others in the family. This includes secrets such as a previous marriage/divorce, a child given up for adoption in the parents' teen years, substance abuse history, mental health diagnoses or treatment, and perhaps most painful of all, sexual abuse. You cannot be authentic when you are keeping big secrets.

It's understandable that topics like these are difficult to talk about, but avoiding them doesn't make things better. Rather, it creates a new problem; when your teen finally finds out about the secret—and they will—they will feel betrayed. Even small secrets can create a sense of insecurity and disconnection. People on the inside of a family shouldn't be on the outside of a big family experience.

An Age-Appropriate Dose of Reality

When families are facing a painful or embarrassing problem, parents understandably want to protect their kids. But sometimes they *can't* be protected, and will experience side-effects in their lives as a result of whatever the problem is. Take missed visits with a father because he has relapsed, for instance. The teen is already experiencing the reality of the problem, so it's important that your teen's realities, along with the underlying problems, are addressed openly and with support. Use the real words—drug addiction, relapse, suicide—don't fear the words themselves. As Dumbledore said: "Fear of a name increases fear of the thing itself." Avoiding talking about something that exists does not protect your teen; it just suggests that they are on their own regarding that problem. Conversely, speaking plainly and openly, and being able to name what something is, allows a child to clearly understand their pain and the origins of that pain, which leads to healing. Look for the reality that your child is already experiencing, and give your child the age-appropriate words to describe their experiences. It can be challenging to know what to say and when, which leads us to the next section: getting support.

Some Conversations Need Support

If your family is wrestling with big, difficult challenges, talking them through with a therapist can be life-changingly supportive. Therapists generally have training in child development, family dynamics, and healthy communication, and have probably had these conversations dozens of times before with other clients. They can role-model how to talk about complex topics and offer support and guidance on how to do it. Therapists come with many different credentials, most commonly: licensed clinical social worker, licensed professional counselor, licensed marriage and family therapist, and licensed psychologist. Working with a professional can make difficult conversations feel and be safer. I'm a big fan of therapy. I'd love to sprinkle it everywhere, but suffice it to say that if your family is facing some of the more challenging "realities," I hope you'll reach out for professional guidance and support. Help is available and it's great to have.

Exercise: Three Buckets

Three Buckets is a tool for helping parents think through what they want to communicate authentically in complicated or controversial conversations. The general idea is to identify three specific perspectives ("buckets") about a difficult topic. Make sure that you are prepared to share information from all three of those perspectives, while of course remembering to build in plenty of time for your teen to share their perspective, too. The perspective buckets are:

1. The facts. In any situation, there are cut and dried facts. Kids deserve to know the truth.

2. Your values regarding those facts.

3. The way your values regarding those facts compare and contrast with the values in other communities that your child will encounter.

Take for example, high school dress codes. The facts are that your daughter's high school has rules about what she can and can't wear, and the administration has the power to pull her from class if her outfit does not fit the rules. Your values about the dress code might be that it is reasonable and appropriate, or unfairly gendered or unfairly enforced. Other communities your child encounters (i.e., other kids, other teachers, her grandparents, local citizens, etc.) will have different positions, which may include supportive or critical messages.

Parents can use the Three Buckets to help themselves think through and clearly communicate what they want to share with their teen on such challenging topics.

REAL-LIFE SCENARIO

Kelly is white and her husband Anthony is Black. Their son Tony is 16 and about to get his driver's license. Anthony has talked with Tony in the past about how to act if they get pulled over by the police, but now that it might happen when Tony is in a car without him, Anthony is really worried. Kelly wants Tony to know his rights and feel secure and confident in asserting them, but she also understands how that might be a dangerous move. This is an issue that deeply needs authentic and effective communication from both parents. Kelly and Anthony discuss what they want to say, and make a plan about how and when to proceed.

The whole family is relaxing in the living room one evening. Kelly speaks up: "You know Tony, we are so excited that you're getting your license next week. We're proud of you

(continued)

for your hard work in driver's ed, and we know you're a good driver." Tony is excited, too, although he plays it cool. Anthony starts to share: "Just being real here, son, it scares the hell out of me to think about you getting pulled over. Driving while Black is dangerous. You're much more likely than a white class-mate to get pulled over, more likely to get searched, more likely to get detained, more likely to get arrested. The cops won't see you as you; they'll see you as a threat. And scared people are dangerous people."

Tony looks like he'd rather be anywhere else, but he's listening.

Kelly chimes in, "I hate that we are having this conversation. I want to tell you that the police are here to protect and serve you as much as anyone, and I want you to know your rights and not let anyone take your power away. But, I know that that per-spective has everything to do with me being white. It breaks my heart to think of any-thing happening to you for any reason, but this seems real and so out of our control—it scares me."

Tony is thinking about how he is scared of being pulled over, but tries to put on a brave face for his parents. He wants to say, "I know, I get it, I understand," but somehow hearing his parents' fear about this is making it even more real. They talk a little longer about being safe, and Tony really listens to his dad when Anthony talks about some of his past experiences with the police, both good and bad. Now that they have had this authentic conversation, the topic is even more open within the family, and they can return to it as needed.

Kelly and Anthony did many things right to make sure this important conversation went well. They talked with each other ahead of time, had a plan, and chose a relaxed, appropriate time to start the conversation. They got straight to the point and kept their portion of the conversation relatively short. Perhaps most importantly, they spoke from the heart, authentically sharing their emotions and perspectives in such a way that Tony could really feel the significance of the situation.

When the eyes say one thing, and the tongue another, a practised man relies on the language of the first.

RALPH WALDO EMERSON, *THE CONDUCT OF LIFE*

CHAPTER 5

KEY SKILL: NONVERBAL COMMUNICATION

The words we speak are powerful, but so are the gestures, facial expressions, and tones of voice we use to say them with. Our body's posture and position add another layer to our messages. Nonverbal communication is mostly learned informally, not consciously. Parents can, however, use an awareness of nonverbal communication to understand their child's signals and to be more effective in their own communication. This chapter includes an extended real-life scenario about disciplining your child in front of his friends.

WHAT IS NONVERBAL COMMUNICATION?

Body posture, position, and proximity; eye contact; facial expressions; hand gestures; and tone of voice all color the messages a person is trying to convey. Sometimes, nonverbal communication is more powerful than words. It can underscore, clarify, mirror, moderate, or invalidate the accompanying words.

REAL-LIFE SCENARIO

Maria's son Ethan has friends over. The boys are in the living room playing video games, when Maria overhears them start to argue. Ethan's friends don't want to play his favorite video game. Ethan raises his voice, everyone starts arguing, things escalate, and then Ethan loses it. He shouts angrily, calls his friends names, and storms off to his room.

Feeling worried, Maria hurries down the hall to his bedroom to talk to him. She thinks she can help him calm down and figure out how to compromise with his friends.

It doesn't work, though. When Maria rushes into his room without knocking, Ethan jerks his head up and yells, "What the hell do you want? Whatever happened to privacy!?" Shocked, Maria throws up her hands in the air and yells back, "Hey! I'm just trying to help you! *Excuuuse* me for trying to make sure you don't lose all your friends!"

It goes downhill from there, with Ethan standing up and yelling to be left alone and Maria yelling about his disrespect. Ethan orders her to get out of his room. Maria can feel her jaw tighten and her hands ball into fists. With her jaw clenched, Maria tells Ethan that because he can't get along with his friends and be respectful to her, everybody needs to go home immediately.

It's also true that nonverbal communication is culturally linked; the meaning of particular nonverbal signals varies between cultures. Eye contact in one culture may be seen as attentive, while in another culture disrespectful, for instance. Still, in many ways, our brains and communication are more basic than we'd like to admit. Jane Goodall said it well: "The chimpanzees taught me a lot about nonverbal communication. The big difference between them and us is that they don't have spoken language. Everything else is almost the same: Kissing, embracing, swaggering, shaking the fist." Teens do have spoken language, but they can be particularly communicative with their nonverbal cues. Think eye-rolling and sarcastic tones. You may not have been explicitly taught how to decode someone's nonverbal signals, but it's absolutely possible and can be very useful.

BODY POSTURE AND POSITION

The ability to accurately interpret—and send—body posture signals is particularly powerful, in part because posture can send a message to a teenager who is mostly not even looking at you. This happens because you and your teen know each other really well. Your child knows your signals *so* well that they can often identify your feelings and overall state with just a glance, sometimes just from posture alone.

A person who is attentive, excited, alert, or agitated is likely to have an activated body posture. This usually involves a straight spine, direct eye contact, and upright head. Conversely, relaxed core muscles, lowered shoulders, and an indirect gaze demonstrate relaxation, disinterest, or even boredom. For example, as Ethan and Maria got increasingly upset with each other, their bodily postures became more activated.

Ethan stood up toward the end of their argument, generally a signal of escalation and often aggression.

These physical signals correspond with the sympathetic nervous system (SNS) and the parasympathetic nervous system (PNS), which are part of how our bodies regulate themselves. When our body is triggered to handle a threat, perform an important task, or take in a critical concept, our SNS helps us do it by making sure that we are alert and ready. And when the need for that readiness is past, we need the PNS to help our body relax, rest, heal, and connect with others. Recognizing the body signals your teenager gives when they are in different nervous-system states helps you tailor your communication to best fit their corresponding emotional state.

Facial Expressions

 Facial expressions communicate enormous amounts of information, such as emotional state, understanding/misunderstanding, agreement/disagreement, or interest/disinterest. Even strangers can gather a lot of information about what you think and feel from facial expressions, and when it comes to one's children, well, there isn't anywhere to hide. Children innately know their parents' facial expressions and what they mean, even down to micro-expressions. It's practically impossible to fool your teenager, despite what you may be saying, if your face says differently. Maria felt shocked, defensive, and angry, and her face surely showed all of those feelings. Beyond the tight jaw, she also likely narrowed her eyes and held tension in her facial muscles, and Ethan would have seen and reacted to every bit of that.

Hand Gestures

Hand gestures can clarify a point, focus the listener's attention, add emphasis, and send signals about the speaker's emotional state. One of my favorite experiences in the therapy room is when sentences get finished with a hand gesture instead of words; it feels synchronous and connected. But too much gesturing, or gestures that are too big, can be distracting and even escalating in moments of stress or conflict. When a situation is increasing in its intensity, someone who comes in waving their arms around is going to heighten the stress level in that room.

When your teen is in an emotional state, the part of the brain that's activated is also the part of the brain that scans for and responds to threats in the environment. Think about a spooked animal that you are trying to approach; most of us know that we should move slowly and not wave our hands about. Your teen is much the same. They had a hard time with the original triggering event, and they may be struggling to balance their own emotional reaction. Things that add to the intensity and overwhelm the situation aren't helpful, whether they are emotional, verbal, or physical. Pointing, making fists, and even just gesturing forcefully are all examples of gestures that are likely unhelpful.

Tone of Voice

Tone of voice involves volume, pitch (how high or low), inflection, and cadence. Most people vary their voice tone relationally and situationally; people speak differently to a young child, a friend, or a spouse, in a presentation at work, when ordering dinner, or when complaining about their team losing. The mood you are in also influences voice tone and gives your teen information about how you are feeling, no matter what you are actually saying.

Specific types of voice tones that can be challenging between parents and teenagers include angry or commanding tones, uptalking, and sarcasm. Some teenagers react instantaneously and negatively to a commanding tone, whereas they might have responded more amenably to a friendly, casual tone. Uptalking—ending a sentence with a lift in pitch—so that the sentence turns into a question, can also be ineffective with teenagers for different reasons. Uptalking can convey a lack of confidence or firmness (for example, when setting a limit), on which teenagers can (will) capitalize. Likewise, the tone of voice that teenagers use with their parents is a common cause of conflict and ruptured communication. Teenagers practically invented disrespectful and provocative tones of voice, and they're a common and powerful trigger for parents.

Sarcasm is a tone of voice with an intent to hurt embedded within it. No wonder the Greek root of the word sarcasm is to "tear flesh." Sarcasm is so powerful that the tone will supplant whatever the message of the spoken words would be; in other words, sarcasm reverses the meaning of those words. Even a fundamentally loving phrase, like "I love you," is hurtful when said sarcastically. Sarcasm is an unhelpful element to have in communication from a parent. But it often stems from hurt, which is good to keep in mind when your teen is being sarcastic with you.

Physical Distance and Touch

 Touch in communication can be very positive, conveying warmth, support, or connection, but it can also convey threat, control, or power. It's important for parents of teenagers to recognize that the teen years see a metamorphosis in how touch and closeness are appropriate and welcome. Most teenagers want their parents to give their bodies more space, at least until *they* want closeness. This is equally true in the way that touch is used in communication. It's generally better not to employ touch in communication when either party is agitated. Consider Ethan and Maria. Imagine if she had walked across the room and put a hand under his arm while telling him to come back out and be with his friends. Touch in that situation would have been incendiary. Parents of teens should make sure to be sensitive to their teen's receptivity for touch in all situations.

Your physical proximity to your teenager also sends a powerful message. Whether it's how close you stand in a particular conversation, or your general presence in their lives, it provides an influential nonverbal cue about your intent, your seriousness, your attention, your timeline, your values, and your expectations. In other words, teens often want a parent nearby, ready to support or engage with when invited, but otherwise they would prefer parents to be about as physically involved as a "potted plant," as psychologist Lisa Damour wryly phrases it.

PUTTING IT INTO ACTION

Now that you understand the backbone of nonverbal communication, let's dive into using those cues effectively to communicate with your teenager. Some elements of nonverbal communication may not feel natural at this point, so I've included concrete action items. This section starts with how to hold your head and your arms, discusses your and your teen's facial expressions (and awareness of and control over them), and then goes on to cover gestures, vocal tone, physical distance, and touch.

Body Posture

 Managing your body posture in a high-conflict conversation can be a powerful nonverbal way to communicate calm to your teen. Start by closing your eyes for a moment and taking a deep breath. Hold that breath for a couple of seconds, then release it slowly. As you exhale, allow your gut to relax, your shoulders to sink, your spine to curve, and your head to tip. Your grandmother might have called this slouching, but I call it purposefully activating our parasympathetic nervous system. Just be sure to recognize that there is a difference between a frustrated exhale and a releasing exhale. Your teenager won't react well to something that sounds like a frustrated huff. The deep breath and slow release can be a helpful de-escalation signal, but only if your exhale is slow and relaxed.

This "slumping" is a micro-intervention that helps your body stay in or return to a state of regulation. In addition, your relaxed body posture signals that your nervous system is calm, which helps your child's lower brain to see the situation as one in which calmness is the right choice. (Please see chapter 6 for more information about regulation and the brain.) It's incredibly powerful to know how to use posture signals from your own body as a de-escalation intervention.

Just a note here on eye contact. Direct eye contact with someone who is upset can intensify situations, which is the opposite of what you want. That is why it's helpful to curve your spine and tip your head; it will lead you to naturally look at the ground or slightly to the side.

Facial Expressions

Do you know when you are making faces? If you aren't sure, ask your teenager—they certainly know! If you can give your child permission to tell you when you are making a face, it will be a huge help for connecting your internal feelings with your external expression. Then, do the cheesy thing and make a few faces in your bathroom mirror. Remember a situation when your teenager told you that you were making a face, or recall a recent situation when you felt frustrated, angry, or distrustful. Your face will likely show a hint of those feelings; notice the details on your face, and connect to how those expressions feel on the *inside*, so that you can notice them more readily next time you make them. Finally, practice calming facial expressions. Start by unfurrowing your brow, unclenching your jaw, and smoothing frown lines. Ask yourself: How can I convey that I am feeling compassion? Neutrality? Curiosity? Empathy? Those emotions, and the associated facial expressions, are generally the most useful ones for handling challenging conversations with a teenager. If you are talking about something delicate, or conflictual, they are probably anticipating your resistance, frustration, or disapproval, so be vigilant that your face isn't conveying those feelings.

Maria, after the fact, wished that she had stopped to take a breath and compose her face into a more relaxed expression. She also recognized that if she had paid more attention to Ethan's face from the start, she might have realized how upset he was. Someone's facial expressions can tell you a lot about their inner emotional experience: Downcast eyes can mean sadness or shame; a jutted-out jaw can mean hurt or defensiveness; drawn lips might signal that someone is trying (and are close to failing) to keep their emotions under control. Your teen's facial expressions will have their own patterns and meanings; be aware of their particular signals, because they offer important information in any communication.

Gestures

Although overactive gestures can be escalating, parents don't need to glue their arms to their sides like a robot. In emotionally escalated situations, be mindful of your hands and body movement. Imagine pulling your energy inward toward your core while simultaneously taking more deep breaths. You might choose not to gesture at all, but if you do, keep your movements slow and close to your chest. Avoid hand gestures that reach far above or away from your core. In line with the "slumped" body posture discussed earlier, consider keeping your hands visible, and open, and your arms uncrossed. Use gestures that are a further expression of that slumped body posture. Make your body movements slow, relaxed, and peaceful. Consider nodding occasionally. Nodding implies alignment, which can help with de-escalation.

Tone of Voice

Both your tone of voice and that of your teenager are very influential in how a conversation is going to play out. Sassy, disrespectful, or provocative tones from a teenager are common triggers for parents. Likewise, teens are sensitive to particular tones of voice from parents. It is difficult to self-monitor, and parents tend to underestimate the level of emotion in their voices. I'm empathetic about this; as a passionate person myself, I know how hard I have to work sometimes to keep my emotions contained.

In general, you can regulate your tone of voice by consciously focusing your awareness on it. I've witnessed a parent speak in an angry and dictatorial tone to his child, saying "absolutely not" and then just minutes later describing his words to me mildly as, "I told her no." I believe that the parent genuinely was not aware of how harsh his tone was, but the effect was still painful.

In order to increase your self-awareness around your tone of voice, try some of the same techniques from the facial expression section: Experiment with different voice tones privately, in the bathroom mirror, or ask your partner or teenager to help you draw your attention to moments when your tone is harsh. Remember, they know what your tone of voice means, even if your words are not consistent with it.

You might also find value in tracking your teenager's different voice tones. Sure, they have one tone that suggests you were born yesterday and can't possibly know anything, but you will find variations that tell you how they are feeling, whether it be frustrated, proud, jealous, embarrassed, desperate, overwhelmed, or hurt. Recognizing tone is an incredibly useful tool to determine when you might need to slow down or change your approach.

Physical Distance

In biology, there is a term called "flight distance" that roughly refers to how close an animal will allow a potential predator to get before it spooks and runs off. We can use the concept of flight distance in parenting, too. Imagine that when your teenager is upset, there is a distance at which they would prefer you to be. How much closeness can they tolerate before it provokes a defensive response or an escalation? This is a moving target because sometimes your proximity is welcome and calming. Other times, it's just not. The goal is to keep a bit of your brain always tracking whether your teen wants you to lean in or lean out. They may signal this with words, or they may use their own physical cues, for example by leaning, walking, or looking away.

Put this into action by recognizing that your actual proximity can and should be varied, according to how helpful it is. Likewise, you can use your physical distance and touch to turn the dial up or down in the intensity and intimacy of your interactions. For example, a touch on the face is more intense; a pat on the shoulder is less so. Standing over someone or leaning over their shoulder is more intense, sitting on their level is less intense, and sitting lower than them is even less intense. Consider each of these variables so you can finely tune your responses for maximum success.

Exercise: Listening to Yourself

Hearing our own varying voice tones can be challenging, but a little technology can help.

1. Choose a word to say aloud using different tones. I find it's easier if the word has more than one syllable. Try your dog's name, your favorite food, or a fun word to say like "zigzag."

2. Turn on your phone's voice recording feature, or just start to record a video with the camera pointing down at the table.

3. Pick an emotion from the list below. Say your word so that it conveys the emotion. Repeat for at least four more emotions.

   - Neutral
   - Happy
   - Sad
   - Worried
   - Irritated

   - Angry
   - Bored
   - Doubting
   - Surprised
   - Compassionate

4. When you're done, listen to the recording. See if you can *hear* the tone. Without looking at the list, can you tell which nuance you were communicating?

5. Play the recording for your partner or your teenager. Ask them if they can label the emotion you were trying to convey with each word. Even if they get remotely close, that's a positive.

REAL-LIFE SCENARIO

Remember Maria from the beginning of this chapter? Her son Ethan got upset; she tried to help, and it exploded. If Maria could have a "do-over" for this experience, she would make some changes, and the story might go like this.

Maria hears Ethan arguing with his friends and then storming off to his bedroom, but she stays seated at her computer for another minute. She remembers how helpful it is to center herself, so she closes her eyes, takes a few breaths, and exhales slowly. Then she checks in with her body and notices tension in her neck and shoulders, so she spends another minute stretching her neck and relaxing those muscles before she calmly gets up, and ambles down the hall to Ethan's room. At the door, she knocks lightly and waits. Ethan responds with a rude-sounding "What?" so she knows to proceed carefully. She takes another breath, tilts her head down and to the side, and composes her face, making sure that her expression is a mix of compassion and empathy, and then opens the door. Standing at the threshold, Maria asks for permission to enter, then notices that Ethan is still holding *his* body very tightly, so she knows to give him plenty of space. Maria shuts the door and sits down on the floor several feet away from Ethan. The whole time she is keeping her muscles relaxed, her gaze mostly averted, and her facial expression soft.

After waiting a few seconds, she speaks, slowly and with a compassionate tone: "That sounded really *frustrating*." This lands well, and Ethan's body relaxes. Maria knows that she will soon be able to speak more, move closer, and make physical contact and eye contact, as he is now de-escalating. She feels that she'll be able to help him think through how to rejoin his friends.

Maria did many things to make this a successful communication with Ethan, largely through the awareness and use of nonverbal communication cues. To make sure that her own sympathetic nervous system wasn't overly activated, Maria:

- Stayed where she was another minute or two.

- Took a few calming breaths.

- Turned her focus inward to her own body when she noticed that her neck and shoulders had tightened up.

- Stretched her muscles. An activated sympathetic nervous system tightens muscles, and purposefully relaxing them can help activate the parasympathetic nervous system.

- Paused to allow her heart rate to slow.

Maria also used these nonverbal communication techniques to de-escalate the situation:

(*continued*)

- "Ambled" down the hallway. Slow footsteps send a much different message than hurried ones.

- Waited at the door before knocking, knocked quietly, and waited. Slow pacing and less intense energy help keep the situation calm.

- Entered Ethan's space slowly and without major body movement.

- Stayed a good distance away from Ethan. The closer you are, the more intense a connection is. Intensity isn't helpful when you are trying to de-escalate.

- Sat on the floor. Even though Maria wasn't threatening Ethan, she knew that his upset brain would still likely perceive threat if she were towering over him.

- Managed eye contact thoughtfully, using less in the beginning, and increasing as Ethan calmed down.

In this version of the conflict, Maria's awareness and use of nonverbal communication cues helped her to help Ethan with his upset feelings; their relationship didn't suffer, and they preserved the evening.

Children feel their parents' emotions exponentially stronger than their parents express them.

CHAPTER 6

KEY SKILL: EMOTIONAL REGULATION

Life can be an emotional roller coaster for parents and teens alike, and strong emotions influence our ability to communicate. Science has made inroads in discovering how the human brain works to manage emotion, and parents can use this information strategically to improve how effectively they communicate in difficult moments. A basic understanding of how brains develop and work, particularly when someone is really upset, is my favorite piece of science to share with you in this chapter. We'll also look at brain development and neuroanatomy, and then learn how to put all of this into effective action. Information that wasn't available a generation ago can do wonders for today's parents, who, to paraphrase Maya Angelou, can know better and do better, thanks to this greater understanding.

REAL-LIFE SCENARIO

Olivia is in 8th grade and has been studying Spanish since she was in elementary school. Her mom, Jessica, has supported and pushed this for Olivia in the hope of helping her gain an advantage for college applications and scholarships. Olivia's high school has a prestigious international studies and languages program that Jessica hopes Olivia will apply to. Instead, Olivia comes home and tells her mom that she is sick of Spanish and wants to focus on her music instead.

Jessica freaks out. She didn't want to let Olivia join the band last year anyway, because what future is there in French horn? Jessica says as much, adding that she knows Olivia only wants to be in the band because her friends are in it. Jessica is thinking about her brother's son, who spent five years in college without graduating. He was too focused on partying, and it scares Jessica every time she thinks about Olivia making similar mistakes. Jessica is upset and keeps lecturing Olivia.

Jessica exclaims, "Why are you so irresponsible! You should be thinking about planning for college."

Olivia rolls her eyes and responds, "All my friends agree that you are the most controlling parent they know."

This is bait, but unfortunately Jessica takes it. She escalates even further and raises her voice, saying, "That's because your friends are lazy, irresponsible slackers who are just going to end up in their parents' basement!"

It's an ugly scene. Olivia ends it, shouting angrily over her shoulder as she stalks off, "OMG, you don't know anything! Don't talk about my friends! I hate you!"

WHAT IS EMOTIONAL REGULATION?

Simply put, emotional regulation is a person's ability to manage their emotions. Emotional experiences happen all day, every day, and they come in a range of flavors. Individuals need to be able to respond to their emotional experiences in effective ways, sometimes by activating, sometimes by holding back. Emotional regulation enables you to prioritize some stimuli over others.

Emotions, especially uncomfortable emotions and our struggles to manage them, lie underneath nearly all difficult behavior. Likewise, challenges with emotions and emotional regulation underpin most parent–child conflicts. Teenagers, in fact all humans, have moments when they lose their ability to tolerate and manage their emotional experiences. The most overwhelming of these moments are what therapists call dysregulation, which is described in greater detail later in this chapter. The chapter begins with a brief overview of brain anatomy, which is the best way to start to understand how to manage the many emotions the brain produces.

Brains Have Different Parts and Different Parts Have Different Functions

Let's start with a review of some neuroanatomy that you've probably heard before. The human brain is divided into three parts: the cerebrum, cerebellum, and the brain stem. Within the cerebrum, there are two hemispheres (left and right) and four lobes (frontal, temporal, parietal, and occipital). The lobes can be further divided into areas, many of which are well-known and often spoken about in the worlds of psychology and human behavior, for example, the amygdala, hippocampus, and the prefrontal cortex. Each of the areas serves specific functions, although understanding the complex interplay between different areas of the brain is still an emerging science. Additionally, the brain receives and sends signals, both chemical and electric, to and from other parts of the body. The different processes of the brain and body are controlled by these signals. This is all background, though; we're about to get to the good stuff.

Brain Development

When babies are in utero, their brains grow from the bottom, up and over, but a newborn infant's brain is far from finished. The brain continues to grow and develop rapidly in early childhood. A six-year-old's brain is about 90 percent of the volume of an adult brain, but it's not until the midtwenties that human brains are considered fully developed. And even once fully developed, it's important to note that brains have what's called neuroplasticity, which means that brains are able to change throughout life by forming and reorganizing connections between neurons.

Generally speaking, the parts of the brain that grow first are more primitive. The brain stem, which controls automatic functions like heart rate and breathing, finishes growing around the end of the second trimester. The cerebellum, which is largely in charge of motor control and coordination, grows rapidly in the third trimester. Importantly however, the cerebrum, and especially the cerebral cortex (the outside layer of the cerebrum, where most of our highest human functioning and thinking happens) is still very immature at birth.

It's important to recognize that the lengthy process of brain development means that our children's brains genuinely don't have the same structural maturity and skills that we do as adults, despite their digital-native status, academic achievement, or frustrating ability to remember random details about when and where we promised them something that we have since forgotten about. Specifically, a part of the brain called the prefrontal cortex is both immature and subject to going offline at times. The prefrontal cortex is the part of the brain that houses most of our highest and best skills, skills that make us human: executive functioning skills, impulse control, emotional regulation, morality, wisdom, planning and organizing, identifying outcomes, and seeing the big picture.

Many of the skills that are housed in the prefrontal cortex are skills that we desperately wish to see in greater frequency in our teenagers. But that's challenging, because the teenage brain does not have a fully developed prefrontal cortex. In addition, adolescence is a time when the brain "prunes" the number of synaptic connections in the prefrontal cortex. In other words, brain functioning in adolescence is not just immature, but also in flux.

The adolescent brain is also affected by hormones. Certainly, parents notice some of the other ways hormones change their teens (puberty! smelly armpits! empty refrigerators!). Brain development is another change. Hormones stimulate growth in certain areas of the brain, including the amygdala. At the same time that the prefrontal cortex is in flux, the amygdala is growing, adding volume and complexity. This translates to emotions, hormones, and impulsivity increasing while wisdom and impulse control are not fully online. The result: The teenage brain.

Dysregulation

The immaturity of the adolescent brain means that even on a good day (meaning their brain is at its best and they are "regulated"), your teenager may not be able to understand consequences, control impulses, and channel a higher morality as well as they will in 10 years. A regulated brain is one that is able to take in stimuli from multiple sources, process and prioritize those stimuli well, and adjust to variable expectations in the environment. Someone who is well-regulated can feel, think, and do. Conversely, imagine what a bad day (or moment) does to the teenager's brain.

When a teenager (or an adult) gets really, really upset, their brain may dysregulate, which means that it has become unable to process input properly. In fMRI scans, which show blood flow to particular areas of the brain, it becomes evident that when a person's brain is dysregulated, their prefrontal cortex turns off; it is less activated, available, and functional. Instead, the *low brain* shows activity, particularly the amygdala and the brain stem. This is incredibly important. It's problematic for our prefrontal cortex to shut off, because that's the part of the brain where impulse control, values, logical reasoning, and problem-solving happens. The low brain is reactive and emotional, much less sophisticated, and is likely to treat the situation as though there is a threat to be handled. This is useful if there is a rattlesnake near your feet; you want your low brain to react quickly and physically: Yes, please jump back! But an argument with your daughter about her desire to quit her dance troupe is not a situation in which an unconscious threat response will be helpful. There is no tiger lurking behind your couch.

Dysregulation brings reactivity, emotionality, and rigidity to the brain and to the interaction. Dysregulation makes you and your beloved teenager lose tempers, overreact, power struggle, yell, make threats, or strike out. It makes people feel threatened and be threatening. More than being unhelpful, it is a nearly unconquerable obstacle to communication. When someone in a situation is dysregulated, true resolution is impossible. Rather, engagement with someone in dysregulation only results in explosions, dominance, or collapse. This is not what you want for your family.

Regulating Ourselves

So, if resolution is impossible in the face of dysregulation, what's a parent to do? The first, and most important step is to check in with yourself. If your teenager is upset to the point of dysregulation, you are probably not feeling your best either. How are your breathing and your heart rate? Do you have any muscles that aren't clenched? Start there. Consider closing your eyes and taking a deep breath, then take another one. Aim to regain your own regulation, or if you managed to stay mostly regulated, aim to bring your nervous system into as calm a state as possible.

I had a moment once when my daughter was around four. We were in the bathroom before bedtime, and she was supposed to be brushing her teeth. She didn't want to brush her teeth, though, and was agitated, grouchy, and tired. She was whining and half yelling and making awful noises, noises that seemed to be boring straight into my eyeballs and brain. I should have given us both a break, but I was dogged in my urgency to get the teeth brushed and the kid to bed. As things progressed—not in a good way—I remember the way my body felt: stiff and tense and alert. And she Just. Kept. Making. Those. Noises. I had this repetitive, hammering thought-loop in my brain that desperately wanted to make her stop the noise by any means possible. I felt as if the inside of my brain were a series of doors slamming, and each one closed off another part of my better brain, leaving me less able to access calm and more and more rigid and desperate. I was dysregulated.

I didn't act violently, but the thoughts were certainly there. I feel lucky that some shred of my higher self was still present. I noticed how rigid and upset I was, and I pivoted on the spot and walked out, toothbrushing be damned. I got myself some space and was able to calm down before I did any damage. This memory has always stood out to me, though, because I could really see how my brain had morphed from mildly tired and frustrated to a state of dysregulation. I was close to making big mistakes. The sensation of rigidity and intensity is memorable to this day.

I use this story with clients sometimes as an illustration of how it might feel to an adult to be dysregulated. While dysregulation isn't an experience that will occur the same way for everyone, I think that the rigidity, intensity, and overwhelm are relatable elements. When we notice those emotions in our own bodies, we need to hang onto a shred of our higher selves and pivot. Dysregulation in a parent rarely turns out well; the best you can hope for is the chance to get some space and calm down. Knowing your own emotional triggers and working to anticipate and manage them is a highly effective prevention technique. Lastly, keep in mind that parents absolutely bear more responsibility in any parent–child conflict. It's the parents' role to be the first to realize the need for a break, the first to check themselves, and the first to repair after a rupture. The adults are responsible for making the first positive move.

PUTTING IT INTO ACTION

Armed with information about brain development and dysregulation, it's easier to understand that, when your teenager is losing it, there is actually a complicated and powerful neurological brain process running in the background. Once parents understand and have internalized that knowledge, and become aware of and find methods to get a handle on their own emotions, they find that they are able to think much more *strategically* and be more effective in their interventions with their teens. Once parents internalize this strategic response, the second goal is to recognize their teen's signals, quickly and accurately.

Triggers

Triggers are the words or experiences that happen immediately before a situation starts to escalate. They may seem to set off the problem, but they aren't always the cause. Situations may have been brewing for a long time, and there may be underlying issues and deeply rooted influences. But the trigger stands out, and it's useful to pay attention to it because it can tell us important information. Jessica was triggered by Olivia's announcement about quitting Spanish, but there were underlying issues, too, such as significant fear about Olivia's future success, and smaller anxieties about the influence of Olivia's friends.

One trigger for many conflicts with teenagers is the teenager being told no. If we know that our teenager is often triggered emotionally by being told no, and we realize that it's a developmentally normal issue (it is), we can approach future "no" moments with a small dose of strategy. Before saying no, for instance, we might verbally acknowledge that we know that they are likely to feel frustrated or mad at us for what we're about to say, for example, "I'm sorry in advance because I know you won't love this, but I'm going to have to say no to that." Having awareness of your teenager's common triggers allows you to be sensitive and strategic in anticipating those triggers, and can often help minimize or prevent escalation.

"HE'S DEAD, JIM."

If you ever watched the original *Star Trek* TV show, you surely heard Dr. McCoy utter that famous line. It's also famous, though less so, as part of a drinking game. The game works like this: While watching *Star Trek*, players take a drink every time something predictable happens, for example, when Dr. McCoy says his dramatic line. With tongue firmly planted in cheek, I offer this as an emotional regulation technique: Certain stressful patterns can be turned into "drinking games."

I'm not actually advising drinking alcohol to cope with your teenager—really, I'm not. Rather, the goal is to use the framework to bring a playful energy to an otherwise triggering pattern. It can be really effective.

The goal is to "play the game" to shift your perspective about small patterns that are emotionally triggering. Whatever the pattern behavior is that is driving you crazy, the game can help you reverse how you relate to it. Each time the behavior happens, you get a point. You can even keep track of your points and treat yourself somehow when you hit a certain number. The result is that instead of dreading or reacting to the behavior, you begin to wait for it with anticipation.

Sarita, mom of three, had a relative who would make passive-aggressive comments about the state of Sarita's house every time she visited. Sarita played the drinking game with respect to the passive-aggressive comments during one visit and discovered that it completely shifted her reaction to them. When before she was triggered, now she was delighted. At the end of the visit, Sarita had "earned" a pedicure, but she told me the biggest reward was the freedom she felt in no longer being so reactive to the passive-aggressive comments.

One caveat—you have to make sure to keep any "drinking game" humor emotionally separate from your child. Otherwise, they are likely to feel as though you are laughing *at* them, which is never helpful.

When Your Teen Is Dysregulated

Beyond triggers, what does your teen look like as they are escalating? What does your teen look like when they are truly dysregulated? Pay attention to their body language and nonverbal communication; it is sending you useful messages when your child is upset. For example, escalation can sound and look like raised voices, tension in voice and body, erect spine, wild gesticulation, and grimacing facial expressions.

When teenagers are dysregulated, parents sometimes try to help, but inadvertently make things worse. A dysregulated teenager is unlikely to calm down if their parent uses verbal interventions like rationalizing, debate, logic, or telling them to calm down. I'll say it more strongly: Verbal interventions usually make things worse with a dysregulated person.

Similarly, when parents themselves co-escalate, or threaten their teenager, the situation often worsens. Really, almost everything a parent tries to do to *make* their teenager calm down is likely to backfire and make things worse. Remember, this is because the part of the brain that is activated and in control is part of the threat detection system in the brain. As the saying goes, when you're a hammer, everything looks like a nail. Your dysregulated teenager's brain will misinterpret almost everything as a further threat and respond accordingly. Your attempt to make them calm down is likely to feel like an invalidation, criticism, or dismissal. The first step when your child is escalating or is dysregulated is for the parent to check themselves. Parents have to keep or regain their own calm to be an asset to the situation.

Techniques for Making Things Better

If your teenager is dysregulated and you have managed to keep your own brain and body regulated, my first response is congrats! Because it ain't easy. Secondly, your calm brain can see, I hope, that your teen is suffering. It may be an offensive, entitled, immature, or selfish display, but it isn't enjoyable for them, either. Remember, too, that it's a neurological and physiological process, and some of what needs to happen just happens naturally. What this means is that your teen's sympathetic nervous system won't stay activated forever. Heart rates slow down; breathing returns to normal; muscles relax. As this happens, their brain begins to re-regulate, too. But this calming will only come about if the "threats" have subsided. And remember, the dysregulated brain sees most stimuli as a threat.

If you're able to stay close-ish, while conveying compassion and/or understanding, you'll find that to be the most effective technique for letting the process run its course with as minimal disruption as possible. To say it another way, when your teenager is dysregulated, your top priority should be to focus on not making things worse, so that the generally hardwired calming process can run its course. Have a calm and nonthreatening body posture and a facial expression that demonstrates compassion and connection. You don't have to do anything; the initial goal is simply to give the physiological process the time it needs to work. It's okay to leave the room or take a break if you need to, but it is recommended that you circle back when you feel calmer. Once everyone is calm, problems, lessons, or reparation can be revisited. When your teenager is dysregulated, do not expect them to be able to have a reasonable conversation with you. The dysregulated brain is best served by giving it the space and time it needs to cool down. Please revisit chapter 5 and the section about non-verbal communication, and especially about flight distance, for support on how to be close in an effective way. Refer to chapter 7 and the section about boundaries for some support in staying close and connected without getting sucked in. And these following techniques have a good track record of helping parents who are trying to manage their emotions and also have the potential (when the time is right) to help teens as well: time, closing eyes, deep breathing, silence, privacy, getting a different physical space, drinking a glass of water, stretching, taking a walk, exercise, rhythm, music, a shower, or mindfulness techniques.

Exercise: Working Backward from Conflict

Think of a recent medium-to-large conflict with your teenager. This exercise will help you identify a few concrete elements of this conflict, enabling you to remain mindful in conflictual situations and to recognize your teenager's triggers and signals. Being able to spot when your teenager's brain is offline is very helpful.

1. Briefly summarize the conflict.

2. Recall the worst part of the conflict. Briefly write what your teenager was saying or doing, then their most upset, worst-behaved moment.

3. What did you say or do immediately *before* that moment?

4. What words or actions were you responding to when you did that? (Notice that we are working backward chronologically.)

5. Can you remember what your teenager was saying or doing before that? Can you remember how they held their body, or if their voice was different (louder, angrier, etc.)?

Many conflicts look alike, so working backward to identify useful information from earlier in one specific conflict is helpful when facing future conflicts or emotional dysregulation. The patterns of interaction between you and your teenager also likely repeat from situation to situation. It's helpful to get fast and accurate at recognizing your patterns and the early signs of escalation so you can intervene early on in a conflict before dysregulation occurs.

REAL-LIFE SCENARIO

Hannah's son Jude is 14. He's been feeling badly about how his body looks as he goes through puberty. Jude finds Hannah one night and tells her that he needs plastic surgery. He is so anxious that he won't look at her, and she can barely make out what he's saying. She finally gets the details: Like many boys still going through puberty, he has a little bit of breast tissue under his nipples. He's certain there's something wrong with him and is ashamed of how he looks. Hannah's heart breaks as he says this, and she feels horrified at the thought of plastic surgery on her son. She rushes to reassure him: "No, Jude, you look totally great! It's normal for boys to have some breast growth during puberty. It's nothing to worry about. Really, it's nothing! I'm sure nobody notices it!"

(continued)

Seeing Jude's shoulders slump as she speaks, Hannah realizes almost immediately that she's messed up. Jude looks unhappy but doesn't say much of anything. Hannah takes a deep breath and stops talking, realizing that she was triggered by Jude's question. She closes her eyes and takes another deep breath, and embraces a moment of quiet. Finally, she can think clearly enough to see what's going on. Jude had to overcome so much to bring this request to her, and her response left him feeling dismissed and belittled. Her upset feelings prevented her from connecting with Jude, resulting in the opposite of what he needed. Thankfully, she catches herself before the situation escalates too far, and Jude's still there, so she gets another try.

Hannah says, "You know what, Jude, I'm so sorry. I jumped right into contradicting you and didn't do a good job listening to you. I won't make you repeat yourself, but can I have a do-over on my reply?"

Jude says, "I guess."

Hannah slowly says, "Thank you. Here's what I wish I had said to begin with. It sounds like this is a really big deal to you. I can tell you are worried and uncomfortable with how your body looks right now." She pauses for a beat before continuing. "I didn't say so originally, and I wish I had, but I do get those feelings. I've had times in my life when I was uncomfortable with how I looked, too, and it's hard. I didn't know you were feeling this way, so I really appreciate that you've brought it up with me."

Jude glances at her for the first time, and she can see that this reply was much closer to what he needed. They talk a little more about his thoughts and feelings, about his body and what it means to him to not look like he wants to, and a little about his hope that plastic surgery would be a fix. This time Hannah stays calm and present, which allows her to be more empathetic and flexible in her thinking. Although plastic surgery isn't an option, she realizes that she doesn't have to convince him of that. Just being able to talk a little about these powerful feelings has brought him relief.

You may think that if you like.

CHAPTER 7

KEY SKILL: BOUNDARIES AND EMOTIONAL BOUNDARIES

WHAT DO WE MEAN BY BOUNDARIES, SPECIFICALLY, EMOTIONAL BOUNDARIES?

Identifying where to set any kind of boundaries with teens is a central challenge for parents, bringing up questions like "Who is in charge here?" and "Whose life is this?" When parents try to answer the first question by giving their teen control, but teens don't do so successfully, it creates emotional turmoil for parents and triggers parents to cross the boundary implicit in the second question. It's very difficult to manage the emotional experience of letting teens "own" their lives when they aren't doing a good job. This chapter includes real-life scenarios with conversations about social exclusion and cultural sensitivity.

REAL-LIFE SCENARIO

Sharon's daughter Asia has a group of friends that Sharon worries about. Sometimes things seem good between the girls, but sometimes Asia gets excluded. Sharon knows about it because she follows the other girls' social media, where they post group pictures showing off how much fun they are having . . . without Asia. It makes Sharon's blood boil and leaves her feeling sick and embarrassed. Sharon herself was on the edge of the popular crowd in high school, and she remembers all too well the anxiety she felt when it seemed she was being pushed out of the crowd.

Lately, Asia's friends have been excluding her again, and Sharon is worried about what to do. When Sharon brings it up, Asia doesn't seem upset, but Sharon can't stop thinking about it. She's sure that the group is only doing it because of one girl, whose mom Sharon knows. Sharon wants to text her, but she did that once before, and Asia got really mad. She's tried giving Asia advice about how to handle the relationships, reminding her to reach out and invite the girls over and how to phrase texts and so forth. Asia got mad about that, too, and pretty much won't talk to Sharon about her friendships anymore. But Sharon finds that she can't get it off her mind. Even though it's her daughter's friend group, it hits Sharon as hard as if it were her own.

An emotional boundary is a psychological delineation between the emotional experiences of two people. The boundary is where one person's feelings stop and the other person's feelings start. Just because you feel angry about something doesn't mean I have to feel angry about it, too. You can be upset about something or even upset with me, and I can still feel regulated. The feelings you have may be important to me, but they are not my feelings . . . even if you are my child. What we are calling boundaries and what we are calling emotional boundaries are entwined. When a parent takes on the emotions of their child, they become embroiled in the child's conflicts and are more likely to become overinvolved in the conflicts and to wrest control from the child.

This chapter will discuss the interaction of boundaries and emotional boundaries, talk about how they affect communication, and offer support for parents trying to manage the emotional experience of allowing their teens to have more control over their own lives.

Emotional Boundaries, Parenting, and Control

How do you typically respond when your teen is experiencing strong emotions? Do you stand back so they can handle it, or do you intervene because they need your help? Do you find it hard to relate to their emotional upset, or do you find yourself feeling upset along with them?

People with truly rigid emotional boundaries will stay far away from their child's emotional experiences and won't be able to relate emotionally to their children. In this situation, a parent is unable to provide the kind of support that will help the child learn to manage their own emotions effectively. It's hard on a child to have a parent with rigid emotional boundaries, and it's likely to leave lasting "bruises" on the relationship and the child's emotional health.

On the other hand, parents with ineffective emotional boundaries may find that their teenager's upset feelings create so much discomfort for them that it becomes intolerable. To manage that discomfort, they may try to take control over the original problem, thereby crossing a boundary. Parents are generally better at predicting outcomes, so sometimes even just the possibility of discomfort is enough to trigger a parent to become overly involved. The parent steps in to control or influence a situation in order to try to prevent bad outcomes. The parent's attempts to increase control are largely due to their own challenges when managing their emotions.

In the scenario at the start of the chapter, Sharon struggled mightily with her own emotional boundaries. The life experiences that her daughter was having triggered Sharon's emotions, both in relation to her daughter's challenges and Sharon's own painful teenage history. Sharon's emotional distress about Asia's issue impaired her communication and hence her relationship with her daughter.

A parent's lack of emotional boundaries with a child's upset feelings can also result in that parent trying to get the child to change their feelings, stop having the feelings, or work through their feelings before they may be ready. This can seem innocuous: "Oh, no, I'm sure it wasn't that bad!" but the messages may be invalidating the teen's feeling in the process. Parents must remember that the teenager's feelings belong to the teenager, and the teen is responsible for their care and keeping.

The "right road" is in the middle. Kids need their parents to be emotionally warm, supportive, and attuned, not enmeshed. Finding the middle ground between "not enough" and "too many" emotional boundaries is key. Managing the boundary between your emotions and someone else's will be a challenge. But the achievement is possible, and parenthood provides abundant opportunities to grow and strengthen your internal emotional boundaries.

Emotional Boundaries and Communication

Healthy emotional boundaries facilitate effective communication. When teenagers know that their parents will practice good boundaries and will allow the teenager to have feelings without those feelings triggering the parent to react in fear or judgment (for example), teens are far more likely to open up to their parents about important or sensitive topics. When parents are overinvolved emotionally or take on the emotions of their children, teens will often push back by shutting the parent out, avoiding discussion, and sometimes lying. Likewise, sometimes teens feel discomfort, overwhelm, or guilt about how their emotions impact their parents, particularly when parents haven't maintained a healthy emotional boundary. When teens feel that their parents have taken on their emotions, holding their parents' emotions in addition to their own can feel burdensome, also hindering communication between parent and child.

Age-Appropriate Suffering

It's your job as parents to help prepare your kids for the real world. Parents typically want to protect kids from the evils and heartbreaks that exist out there. That's normal and healthy and generally encouraged. But the other very important job is to help children acquire the skills, habits, resources, and strengths to be able to handle the problems of the world on their own. In order to do this, you've got to allow kids to have a dose of the reality of the world, even when it's an ugly reality.

Sometimes parents do this by making sure that they don't overprotect their kids from age-appropriate stressors. For example, most adolescents master the necessary habits to care for their own body. The 13-year-old who hasn't quite internalized your years of reminders doesn't need you to protect him from the consequences of his stinky armpits. Rather, just a single, small dose of age-appropriate reality (i.e., disdain from a peer) will likely provide the push toward better hygiene.

Keep in mind that suffering has value, and that there is both "age-appropriate stress" as well as "too much stress." Parents who have loose emotional boundaries have a hard time letting their children "suffer." Nevertheless, preventing age-appropriate stress or trying to taking it on oneself robs kids of an opportunity to grow. Likewise, parents with rigid emotional boundaries may fail to appropriately support their child emotionally when stressors are too weighty. If finding a place of healthy balance is a challenge for parents, it can be helpful to engage a therapist.

PUTTING IT INTO ACTION

Knowing about boundaries and emotional boundaries is one thing; maintaining them in a healthy way is another thing entirely. This section offers concrete techniques and advice that parents can use to make emotional boundaries easier to set and hold. Recognizing patterns helps parents use preventative and strategic techniques. Prioritizing your own regulation is key for staying connected with the best part of your brain, and out of the threat-response part of your brain. Recognizing what you can and can't (and shouldn't try to!) control helps keep relationships and situations peaceful and positive, and boundaries easier to hold. Avoiding arguing with teens is difficult but necessary.

Recognize the Patterns

Hard moments in a family often occur in repeated patterns. Certain times of day, triggers, situations, or topics may tend to create tension or conflict. Recognizing them is a proactive step that will allow a parent to maintain their emotional boundaries more easily and effectively. As discussed in chapter 6, predicting challenges gives us emotional space and perspective around those patterns. If you see the challenge coming, you can identify and practice a method for better coping with it.

The next time you have a challenging situation, pay attention to details. As soon as you can, write down some of the details. Notice vulnerable situations, typical triggers, and any customary signs that your teenager is escalating. Over time, you'll notice in your notes that many elements get repeated, which is helpful for early identification. The earlier you can spot a difficult or escalating situation, the better. Earlier intervention is more effective, for many reasons, not the least of which is that everyone's brain is likely to be more regulated, so you are less likely to lose the boundary between your own emotions and your teen's.

It could have been a big help for Sharon to recognize that anytime Asia had "frenemy" problems, it was likely to be emotionally triggering for Sharon herself. Realizing that would allow her to make preventive choices, like not following Asia's friends on social media or being conscious about the need for a brief, reflective pause if/when the issue showed up. Sharon might also have found it helpful to talk with her therapist about how to better disentangle her feelings from Asia's.

Prioritize Your Regulation

When your teenager gets upset, their upset can trigger your own. Being upset makes it harder to think clearly, to set and hold healthy emotional, and therefore other boundaries, and to have effective communication. This merits a quick reminder about the advice in chapter 6 on emotional regulation. In situations in which your emotional boundaries are tested, focus first on maintaining or regaining your own regulation. Close your eyes. Take that deep, slow breath and let it out peacefully, relaxing the muscles in your core, shoulders, and jaw as you do. Take a break if you need one. Prioritize your sense of calm, safety, and regulation. From that point forward it will be easier to hold your emotional boundaries.

The Velvet Rope

Imagine a velvet rope, the kind you might see at an old-fashioned theater, hung in a swag between two brass posts. The velvet rope is my favorite visual metaphor for an ideal type of boundary between parents and teens. We don't want a brick wall or a chain link fence as the template for our boundary, but we do want a clear, healthy delineation. Our emotions are ours, and our teen's emotions are theirs: theirs to deal with, theirs to struggle with, conquer, and learn from. If your teenager unhooks that velvet rope and invites you over, metaphorically speaking, you can choose carefully if and how to do that. Sometimes more involvement is warranted in our teenager's emotional lives, and it can be loving and helpful. The key is to be able to recognize those moments accurately, and to proceed judiciously. The next time you find yourself in a place of challenging emotional boundaries, for example, if your teen is experiencing something mildly painful, picture the velvet rope in your mind. Use the image to guide you in how to manage the boundary. Allow the image to help you remember to be present and compassionate, but emotionally separate and not in charge of fixing your child's emotional challenge.

The Wisdom to Know the Difference

A legacy from generations past is the belief that parents can and should have significant control over their children, in a variety of ways: behaviorally, emotionally, morally. But the world has changed; personal freedoms are more widespread, and parents have come to recognize that control over one's teenager is a dubious goal. You can, and should, however, create the kind of mutually respectful relationship with your teenager in which you have influence. Influence is vastly different from control. Healthy boundaries permit us to influence and be influenced, especially by people we love. Parenting with influence requires that we are aware of our important values, and don't try to use our influence when it isn't important or appropriate.

As with the suggestions in the chapter on authentic communication, a little introspective work is helpful here. What are your most important values? Are you role-modeling them consistently? Hopefully the answer is yes, and if so, you can rest assured that you have already done the most important thing a parent can do to influence their child in positive ways. The ways in which your child is different from you, or areas in which they are underperforming, are not places where you should automatically step in and take charge. Sometimes a teenager will welcome your help, but it should be a mutual decision for you to be in charge of some part of their life. It should not be a point of conflict. Don't get bogged down in immediate challenges and failure. Keep your eye on the long-range goal: growth that produces an adult who is capable of managing their own healthy, happy life.

Lastly, when it comes to controlling our children, I love this quote from Shefali Tsabary: "We cannot control our children. We can only create the conditions for them to rise."

Don't Bring in the Lawyers

Some days it seems as if parents need to be professionally trained litigators to beat their teenager in an argument. The problem with that is that, just by arguing with your teenager, *they win*. If you're arguing, they're winning. It's hard to stop, for sure: They know you, your sensitive buttons, and your passions, plus they have the ability to use your emotions against you. Healthy boundaries require a parent to be able to firmly and gracefully exit an argument when needed.

Resist the need to control or the need to convince your teen to agree with you. Instead, practice this mantra, "You may think that if you like." Arguing with teens isn't likely to convince them either to agree with you or to do what you want on the larger issue. Instead, it's likely to strengthen their opposition. Take a deep breath, use effective nonverbal communication, don't argue, hold your emotional boundaries, and give yourself permission to take a break if you need one. It's fine for teens to "get the last word" if that's what it takes to end an argument. The following quiz will help you identify your strengths and weaknesses in maintaining emotional boundaries in your relationship with your children.

Quiz

1. I have a hard time being consistent—I regularly don't follow through with my limits or consequences.

   1. Practically Never
   2. Rarely
   3. Sometimes
   4. Usually
   5. Almost Always

2. I find myself in arguments with my child about my limits and expectations.

   1. Practically Never
   2. Rarely
   3. Sometimes
   4. Usually
   5. Almost Always

3. I am very flexible and patient to a point, but when I feel that I have been pushed too far, I tend to lose it.

   1. Practically Never
   2. Rarely
   3. Sometimes
   4. Usually
   5. Almost Always

(continued)

4. My child's emotional reactions are generally predictable and make sense to me.

   1. Almost Always
   2. Usually
   3. Sometimes
   4. Rarely
   5. Practically never

5. I have good insight about my own inner emotional life and allow myself to feel a wide range of emotions.

   1. Almost Always
   2. Usually
   3. Sometimes
   4. Rarely
   5. Practically Never

6. I am able to regulate my emotions most of the time, and I don't take it personally when my teenager acts up or is disrespectful. It's rare that I lose my cool with my teenager, and when I do, I circle back later to repair the relationship.

   1. Almost Always
   2. Usually
   3. Sometimes
   4. Rarely
   5. Practically Never

Scoring: Questions 1–3

High scores are 10 and above. Low scores are five and below. The **lower** your score in this category, the more likely it is that you parent with consistency and boundaries. This is a positive influence for relationship strength and effective communication. Just keep an eye on not letting your tendency for consistency creep into too much structure or control.

If your score is **high** in this category, you may find that your ability to hold effective limits with your teenager isn't where you want it to be. Your teen may know that what you say isn't very meaningful, although they may be afraid of you losing your temper.

Scoring: Questions 4–6

High scores are 10 and above. Low scores are five and below. The **lower** your score in this category, the more likely it is that you have high "EQ." EQ refers to emotional intelligence, and it's a set of skills that allow us to recognize emotions in ourselves and others, to communicate more effectively, to regulate ourselves, and to maintain emotional boundaries. Some parents "inherit" EQ skills, but others make a conscious effort to acquire them.

If your score is **higher** in these three questions, you probably did not get support or maybe not even permission to feel your feelings during your own childhood. You might find it helpful to read Daniel Goleman's book *Emotional Intelligence* or, even more powerfully, to work with a therapist to rediscover your inner emotional life and build skills for better relationships and happiness.

REAL-LIFE SCENARIO

Xiaohui is 13, and comes home from 8th grade one day looking especially low energy. Her mom, Karen, wonders if something is wrong and asks her. Xiaohui tells her that her 7th period teacher won't say her name. Xiaohui says that, on the first day of school, her teacher called roll and when she got to her name, called out "Ms. Thompson" even though she had called all the other kids by their first names. Xiaohui explains, "I raised my hand and said, 'My name is pronounced Xiao-hui, sh-ow, rhymes with wow, and hui is pro-nounced like way.' And Ms. Smith just shook her head once really quick and said, 'I'll call you Ms. Thompson.' And she has. Every day, she calls me Ms. Thompson, but all the other kids she calls by their first name."

Karen is incensed. Really, really mad. First of all, she recognizes this as a microaggression, or more specifically, a microinvalidation. Secondly, she can't believe that her daughter (bravely!) advocated for herself and the use of her given name, and the teacher refused it. She feels her heart rate speed up and her nostrils flare. But she closes her eyes for a second and takes a deep breath.

Karen and Xiaohui have faced this before; a version of it every year, sadly. When Xiaohui was in elementary school, Karen learned to reach out to teachers ahead of time, sending the phonetic pronunciation via email, but since Xiaohui began middle school, she hasn't wanted her mother to get involved. Karen very much wants to help, but she knows that Xiaohui is unlikely to want her to intervene. She takes another deep breath to calm herself a little more, and begins speaking—with compassion—to Xiaohui: "Oh boy. Here we go again. Seems like there's always one. I'm sorry, kiddo, I know that's hard on you." She pauses briefly. "When you were telling your story, I imagined myself bursting into her classroom shouting about microaggressions and maybe bringing a Power-Point on the responsibility of teachers to make students feel welcome ... but ... I bet you want me to let you handle it your way, huh?"

Xiaohui rolls her eyes slightly at the PowerPoint comment. "Yes, mother. I can handle this. I don't want you to get involved."

Karen hugs her and says, "You *can* handle it. I know you can. I'm glad you told me what happened. We are here for you if you ever decide that you do want our help."

CHAPTER 8

PUTTING IT ALL TOGETHER

This chapter focuses entirely on the wisdom of other parents, with lessons and stories all drawn straight from real life. The first section is about meaningful lessons that I have learned from parents. The second section of the chapter includes stories from four different families, as the parents try to manage difficult communication issues with their teenagers, using active listening, authenticity, nonverbal communication skills, emotional regulation, and healthy boundaries. The scenarios in this chapter include topics such as ADHD, substance abuse, checked-out teens, the college experience, household chores, and sexuality on social media.

LESSONS PARENTS TAUGHT ME

Here are examples of some of the many lessons I have learned throughout my time in practice, including one parent's successful technique for emotional regulation and another parent's poignant realization about the limits of her ability to protect her daughter.

I Just Took Away My Permission to Lose It

Kevin's son Jayden (13) had been through a lot in his life: his mom's addiction, parents' divorce, several moves in the last few years, and a recent diagnosis of ADHD. He'd also been going through some difficult challenges at school lately, and it was showing up in difficult behavior at home. Almost every night, Kevin found himself frustrated and pushed to his limits by Jayden's distracted and irritable behavior. It didn't help that Kevin was also going through a hard time, with financial worries and work stress. Kevin felt himself "caving in" to his frustrations almost daily, escalating, yelling, and making threats. He would try to stay calm and talk things out with Jayden, but after a few minutes of trying to stay calm, it would seem pointless and he'd let go into his anger. Afterward, he'd feel guilty and knew he was just making things worse.

We talked about the pattern many times, and he understood what was going on with Jayden (who was exhausted, overwhelmed, and feeling shame about school). He knew what Jayden needed from him: a safe space to vent and even work out all the unmanageable emotions from his day (and old stuff, too). Kevin wanted to support his son that way, but kept finding himself upset and yelling.

One day he came in for a session and told a different story. That week, when Jayden was being distracted, Kevin stayed calm. He replayed the scene and talked about how he just kept his temper, waited calmly, and didn't react when Jayden was grouchy and difficult. He also described having made some changes at work so that he could be more present at home. I asked what was different, and he said, "I removed my permission to let myself sink so low. I can't let myself or my energy sink so low, especially in how I react to Jayden. It isn't okay, and I can't let myself do it anymore."

At the time, I wondered whether it would stick. But it did. Kevin made a significant shift in how he handled those moments, and although nothing is ever perfect, he generally stayed true to his new expectations of himself from that point forward. He had truly "removed permission to sink so low."

I thought about it once a couple of years ago in the middle of my own rough parenting moment. Ironically, it came into my mind right after I gave myself permission to be testy and irritable with my child. I was tired and annoyed and didn't want to take the high road . . . and I didn't. Immediately after, here came Kevin's memory, reminding me of what I *should* have done. (Heavy sigh.) Perhaps you can find something in this story for yourself. For me, I know that I can give myself permission to do many things, but I try not to let losing my temper be one of them.

I Can't Save Her from Herself

Nisha's daughter was 17 and about to come home from the residential treatment program where she'd just spent 60 days in treatment for substance abuse. Nisha spent many of those weeks adjusting to the loss of control that checking your daughter into a treatment facility brings but had been feeling panicky ever since the family therapist told her that her daughter was nearing discharge. Nisha had a spreadsheet of appointments, arrangements, and tasks to manage before her daughter came home. Nisha had been working through the spreadsheet steadily, taking care of one responsibility after another, trying to make things perfect. But that day, problem-solving didn't seem to be helpful. Our conversation shifted back to the stress she was feeling, and I wondered aloud about boundaries.

We talked about it for a while, and eventually Nisha said, "I know what the real problem is here. I don't want it to be true, but it is. I can't save her from herself. If she wants to be a drug addict, I can't stop her."

Parents of older teenagers often have a hard time letting go of a particular piece of control: allowing their kid to mess up. Nisha's daughter had already messed up a lot. She was truly at risk of making mistakes that would affect her negatively for the rest of her life. This was no small thing to let go of.

And yet, it wasn't possible for Nisha's daughter to feel capable of managing her own life as long as her mom was unwilling to let her try. If Nisha's fear, however well-founded, continued to cause her to cross the boundary and take responsibility for her daughter's sobriety, her daughter wasn't ever going to take that responsibility on herself, a responsibility necessary for maintaining sobriety.

It was the scariest, and riskiest, realization Nisha had ever made, but once she did, it made all the difference. She began to treat her daughter more independently, offering support instead of control and supervision. She made it clear that she was available to help her daughter in any way her daughter wanted, but she left the decisions and the parameters up to her daughter. Her daughter came home from rehab and, with lots of personal and professional guidance, they crafted a support plan together. Their relationship continued to heal and grow, and to Nisha's everlasting relief, her daughter remained sober.

WORKING THROUGH IT

In situations big or small, unusual or mundane, these skills can make a tremendous difference. There's a lot to remember and consider in challenging communication situations. Regulating our own emotions, active listening, nonverbal communication, being true to ourselves, and managing boundaries . . . it's a lot. The following stories are illustrations of how parents have put it into practice in their own lives. The common threads in many parenting-teenagers success stories are the parents' calm, an understanding of and compassion for their teen's perspective, and healthy boundaries. You'll see those truths in the following stories. Happily, a life-long relaxed temperament isn't required; as parents we are *all* growing.

Eric and Henry

One evening, as Eric is in the kitchen working on dinner, he asks his son Henry to come help. Very begrudgingly, Henry puts his phone in his pocket and shuffles into the kitchen. Eric is making stir-fry and asks Henry to manage the food in the pan while he dices more vegetables. Henry picks up the spatula, gets his phone back out, and begins half-heartedly stirring dinner while still scrolling. Eric immediately feels perturbed. Sautéing chicken isn't that hard, but you do have to look at it to do it properly, and it bugs him that Henry won't put down his phone for five minutes. Eric takes a deep breath and imagines several ways this situation could play out:

1. Bark at Henry to put his phone away and pay attention to what he's doing. Last time he did that, they got into a shouting match that ended with Henry yelling "Fine! I don't even *want* this dinner! I'm not eating!" as he stomped out of the kitchen to his room. Eric is trying to avoid these types of shouting matches, and he knows the barking is his default setting, so he's actively trying *not* to do that.

2. Avoid conflict. Eric could not say anything; Henry would continue to stare at his phone and half-heartedly stir dinner. Eric knows he's likely to just keep stewing, which might lead to a fight later about something else.

3. Wait a minute and then try to draw Henry into a conversation about something unrelated. Eric remembers that Henry had a presentation in US history that day

and thinks that he might respond well to being asked about that.

Eric takes another regulating breath and, while chopping veggies, casually asks Henry about the presentation. He keeps his voice light and relaxed and says nothing about the phone. Henry mumbles his first reply, but Eric is able to keep himself regulated and just asks a follow-up question, which does a better job of drawing Henry in. Henry doesn't turn the phone off, but he sets it down and Eric can feel the conversation getting more interactive. He high-fives himself mentally.

Eric feels that this story is a little victory, but I think it was a huge victory: Thinking about and choosing a reaction, and getting a positive result, is a BIG deal, especially when you're just learning to do it. Specifically, Eric's conversation went well because he:

- Thought through how he wanted to react (emotional regulation, authenticity)

- Kept his voice light and continued to work on dinner (nonverbal signals that it wasn't a problem/conflict/ "threat" situation)

- Withheld judgment and asked questions about Henry to draw Henry into connection (active listening and being attuned to what Henry is likely to be interested in/feeling/open to connecting about)

Amanda and Emma

Amanda and Julie have two daughters: Emma and Lucy. They are proud of their daughters; they are both great students with healthy relationships and lots of interests. Nevertheless, Amanda worries about 16-year-old Emma sometimes, because Emma doesn't really share a lot about what's going on in her head or in her life. Amanda wants more conversation, more overlap, more connection, but has noticed that she has to be very careful to walk a fine line between being interested, but not *too* interested, or else Emma will shut down. Specifically, if Amanda asks too many follow-up questions or seems too excited, Emma will end the conversation.

One weekend, as the family is driving to visit relatives a couple of hours away, Emma comments that she's been looking at colleges online. Amanda instantly feels excited and apprehensive. This is a big conversation, one that she feels excited and happy about, and college is so important, but she immediately recognizes this as one of those tricky situations. She takes a deep breath and thinks about her options:

1. The usual, old way: Amanda, trying to show Emma how excited and supportive she is, being too enthusiastic, asking too many questions. Emma will stop talking, and Amanda will see a shadow pass over her daughter's face as she closes up. Amanda remembers how painful and frustrating this experience is for her and reinforces her resolve to *not* let it go this way today.

2. Careful, connected interaction: Emma is opening up to Amanda about something important. Amanda takes a deep breath and reminds herself that she wants this to be the first of many conversations about this topic and that Emma gets overwhelmed with too much enthusiasm.

It only takes a split second of that awareness to remind Amanda how best to proceed. She pauses, centers herself physically, relaxes her chest and stomach, and reminds herself to manage her nonverbal signals. She keeps her voice pitched normally, and tries to use voice inflection that reflects the emotional boundaries that she knows Emma prefers. And then she nails it: Sounding relaxed, moderately interested, and patient, Amanda replies, "Oh yeah? Anything interesting?"

Success! Emma keeps sharing. She talks about where she's looking and what she likes and doesn't like about what she sees. Amanda never utters a word the whole time and is delighted by how much Emma opens up. When it seems that Emma has reached the end of what she wants to say, Amanda asks just one question. Again, Amanda makes sure to modulate her voice tone, pace, and inflection to keep it casual. It helps, too, that they are in the car and are both looking out the windshield instead of at each other. Emma talks a little longer in answer to the question, and Amanda again waits a bit and then simply says, "Thanks for telling me all that, Em."

Amanda does have more questions she wants to ask but recognizes that it works better for Emma to get a break, so she plans to circle back in a day or two, with one follow-up question at a time. Amanda is so grateful that this conversation went well, and doubles down on her commitment to "keep it casual."

Note that Amanda's success was made possible by:

- Careful emotional regulation (excitement is a big emotion; one that her daughter is particularly sensitive to)

- Great emotional boundaries (allowing Emma lots of space in the interaction to have her own emotions)

- Savvy nonverbal cues (sending body and vocal signals that underscore her calm and boundaries)

- Conversational pacing (another nonverbal technique that allows Emma to have more control over the conversation and feel more comfortable)

Robin and Aiden

Robin is cleaning house one Saturday afternoon. Her 15-year-old son Aiden is in his room with the door open. He's wearing headphones and gaming online with friends. She waves to get his attention, and he pulls his headphones away from his ears and glances at her.

She says, "Hey Aiden, I need you to unload the dishwasher and get your clothes out of the dryer, okay? Also, your lunchbox is still sitting on the counter from yesterday, so pretty please deal with that and put it away."

Aiden gives a half-nod, and the headphones snap immediately back into position. An hour later, Robin heads to the laundry to wash sheets and fold the towels and finds that Aiden has done absolutely nothing. She has been cleaning the whole house the entire time. She feels resentful and agitated. Why on earth is it okay for him to play games all day while she works? The angry voice in her head ramps up, with thoughts about "entitlement" and "when I was his age, I never..."

But first, Robin sits down for a minute and gives herself some space to breathe and think. Are these chores reasonable? Yes. Has Aiden had a chance to do his own thing today? Yes. Did he really hear her request earlier? That's iffy. His brain was surely still mostly on the game when she was speaking to him. Is he responsible for the fact that she is feeling overworked and frustrated right now? Not really. Does he usually do what she asks? Yes.

This conversation with herself is helpful, and she feels calmer. Robin reminds herself that a lot of her feelings are more about herself and her experiences than this specific moment of Aiden's behavior. But he does need to do those chores, because their family values are that everyone contributes to the running of the household.

Robin recognizes that her anger won't help the situation but that a firm limit is appropriate. She thinks about what she's going to say and do, centers herself, takes another deep breath, and goes into Aiden's room. This time, she asks him to pause his game and pull the headphones all the way off. Once she has his full attention, she reminds him of the earlier request, the time that has already elapsed, and states simply that the chores can't wait any longer, particularly the clothes, because other items need to run through the machine. She throws in an empathetic statement: "I'm sure it's annoying to you that I keep interrupting your game, and I am sorry about that. But sometimes the chores can't wait, and this is one of those times. Come on in there with me now, and I'll help you get started."

Aiden was so immersed in his game the first time that he really had no idea that an hour had elapsed. He appreciates how chill his mom is being about that, and especially that she's going to help him get started. He stands up, and they work together for a while. Things feel good between them; they chat while they work, and Aiden puts effort into what he's doing.

Robin did many things right in this situation, including:

- Calming her body and her mind before going in to speak with Aiden (emotional regulation)

- Thinking through the big picture and not overfocusing on one event (emotional regulation, boundaries, and authenticity)

- Recognizing that some of her upset emotions were more about her own stuff than what Aiden was doing/ not doing (emotional boundaries)

- Making sure she had his full attention before the second conversation (nonverbal communication and active listening skills)

- Staying true to her values about everyone in the family contributing to the running of the house, while being a little flexible in the moment (authenticity and boundaries)

Melissa and Emily

Melissa's daughter Emily is 17. Melissa gets a text one night from her close friend Suzanne, who happens to be the mother of Emily's BFF. Suzanne says that she just heard that there are inappropriate pictures of some of the girls in their daughters' class that are being shared on social media. Melissa immediately begins to feel a sense of panic creeping up inside; is Emily involved?

Melissa thinks for a minute about her values. She reminds herself that teenagers are famous for impulsive decisions, and she reminds herself that she is more concerned about privacy than about sexuality. Most importantly, Melissa reminds herself that even if her daughter is involved in any way, Melissa's role is to be a helper, *not* to make her feel worse about it. Melissa takes a deep breath, stretches to loosen up her body a little, and goes to find Emily.

She knocks on Emily's door. Emily is at her desk, so she sits in the low chair nearby. Melissa takes another good breath and dives in: "So, I just got a text from Suzanne. She's worried because apparently there are some inappropriate photos of girls in your class that are being passed around on social media. Can we talk about this?"

Emily knows all about these photos and knows this isn't going to be a fun conversation, but she agrees to talk. Melissa digs a little deeper: "Would you tell me what you know?"

Emily admits that she's seen some of the photos. Yes, someone sent her one. No, she didn't forward it; she deleted it.

Melissa wants to lecture and shriek about why Emily didn't talk to her about this already but keeps her mouth shut and focuses on really listening to what Emily says. Melissa also remembers to keep her body as relaxed as possible. When she talks, she keeps her voice low and slow. "I do have a couple of concerns. Will you hear me out?" Emily nods. "Seventeen is underage and taking or sharing these photos might be breaking federal law. I'm especially worried for the girls in the photos, but also for you if you have participated in any way."

Emily agrees and says, "I know, Mom, but I already said I wasn't involved. I deleted the one I got, and I hope you don't think I'm dumb enough to take a photo like that."

Melissa responds, "Okay, you're telling me that you've seen them, but you weren't actively involved in any way. You've made choices to mostly stay out of the situation. I'm not surprised—you do have good boundaries; I know that."

Melissa pauses and notices that Emily appreciates the acknowledgment. She continues: "I appreciate you talking with me about this. I'll just say one more mom-thing and then I will zip it on the advice. I know I've said a million times that stuff on the internet never dies . . . nude photos are the worst of that. They can get uploaded to a share site and be seen by people all over the world for the rest of someone's life."

It's true, most of what Melissa says is stuff that she's said before, but Emily is really listening now. She wasn't thinking of the lifelong consequences before Melissa brought that part up. They talk a little longer about what to do from there, and both of them are happy to have a calm conversation about the situation.

Melissa's conversation with Emily went as well as it did in part due to her planning and choices:

- She stopped to remember her true values and goals (authenticity).

- She paused before responding, calmed herself, and released tension in her body ahead of the talk (emotional regulation).

- She sat low, kept her body relaxed, and spoke low and slow (nonverbal signals).

- She stayed in a listening role, not rushing through to say her piece, not lecturing, withholding judgment, and reflecting back what Emily said, especially after Emily said it the second time (active listening).

- She asked for permission several times: to talk, to go deeper, and to share her opinions and thoughts (boundaries).

A FINAL NOTE

If you're reading this, you've probably just finished the book. Congratulations! Reading an entire parenting book (or even part of one) is no small feat. It's a reflection of the high value you place on your family and your parenting. It's been my honor to share this parenting advice with you, and I truly hope that you've found insight and support in these pages.

Thank you for reading!

FURTHER RESOURCES

BOOKS

The Whole Brain Child by Daniel J. Siegel, MD, and Tina Payne Bryson, PhD

A very readable explanation about how brains work related to emotion and behavior; if you only read one, make it this one.

Brainstorm by Daniel J. Siegel, MD

One of the same authors as *The Whole Brain Child* but with a specific teen focus.

Getting to Calm by Laura S. Kastner, PhD, and Jennifer Wyatt, PhD

A wonderful, topic-based guide for parents of teens.

How to Break Up with Your Phone by Catherine Price

Ways to create a "relationship" with our smartphones in which the phones serve us, not the other way around.

What Happened to You by Bruce Perry and Oprah Winfrey

Fabulous balance of brain science and great storytelling. I would love everyone to read this book.

Out of Control: Why Disciplining Your Child Doesn't Work, and What Will by Shefali Tsabary

Deep truths, presented with strong language—put on your thick skin before reading.

Full Catastrophe Living by Jon Kabat-Zinn

On mindfulness.

Mindfulness Workbook for Beginners by Peter Economou, PhD

A great place to start with mindfulness.

"Family Media Plan," from the American Academy
of Pediatrics.
HealthyChildren.org/English/media/Pages/default.aspx

American Academy of Pediatrics site with resources and guidance for regulating your children's screen time.

Sean Fargo's Mindfulness Meditations (audio)
MindfulnessExercises.com/teacher/sean-fargo

Guided meditations to improve your mindfulness.

Insight Timer App

Free app for meditation.

REFERENCES

CHAPTER 1

American Psychological Association. "APA Review Confirms Link between Playing Violent Video Games and Aggression." August 13, 2015. APA.org/news/press/releases/2015/08/violent-video-games.

Anderson, Monica, and Jingjing Jiang. "Teens, Social Media & Technology 2018." Pew Research Center: Internet, Science & Tech, May 31, 2018. PewResearch.org/internet/2018/05/31/teens-social-media-technology-2018.

Kamenetz, Anya. "Screen Addiction Among Teens: Is There Such a Thing?" NPR, February 5, 2018. NPR.org/sections/ed/2018/02/05/579554273/screen-addiction-among-teens-is-there-such-a-thing.

Kelly, Yvonne, Afshin Zilanawala, Cara Booker, et al. "Social Media Use and Adolescent Mental Health: Findings from the UK Millennium Cohort Study." E Clinical Medicine. *The Lancet*, January 4, 2019. TheLancet.com/journals/eclinm/article/PIIS2589-5370(18)30060-9/fulltext.

CHAPTER 2

American Academy of Pediatrics. "Family Media Plan." HealthyChildren.org. HealthyChildren.org/English/media/Pages/default.aspx

Chen, Ping, and Kathleen Mullan Harris. "Positive Family Relationships and Mental Health from Adolescence to Midlife." *JAMA Pediatrics*. JAMA Network, October 7, 2019. JAMAnetwork.com/journals/jamapediatrics/fullarticle/2752557.

Runcan, Patricia Luciana, Corneliu Constantineanu, Brigetta
Ielics, et al. "The Role of Communication in the Parent-Child
Interaction." *Procedia: Social and Behavioral Sciences.*
ScienceDirect, 2012. ScienceDirect.com/science/article/pii
/S187704281201350X/pdf?md5=38864ba888e7e3b0e92fa936
8997a08f&pid=1-s2.0-S187704281201350X-main.pdf.

CHAPTER 3

Ebbert, Ashley M., Frank J. Infurna, and Suniya S. Luthar. "Mapping
Developmental Changes in Perceived Parent-Adolescent Relationship Quality throughout Middle School and High School:
Development and Psychopathology." Cambridge Core. Cambridge
University Press, October 25, 2018. Cambridge.org/core
/journals/development-and-psychopathology/article
/abs/mapping-developmental-changes-in-perceived
-parentadolescent-relationship-quality-throughout-middle
-school-and-high-school/5E8E3AA15FB305E9F7C5E
297F1E109EB.

Lantos, Hannah, Jennifer Manlove, Elizabeth Wildsmith, Bianca
Faccio, Lina Guzman, and Kristin A. Moore. "Parent-Teen
Communication about Sexual and Reproductive Health:
Cohort Differences by Race/Ethnicity and Nativity." *Interna-
tional Journal of Environmental Research and Public Health.*
MDPI, March 7, 2019. NCBI.NLM.NIH.gov/pmc/articles
/PMC6427285.

Laursen, Brett, and W. Andrew Collins. "Parent-Child Communication During Adolescence." *Handbook of Family Communication.*
Accessed July 8, 2021. ResearchGate.net/profile/Brett-Laursen
/publication/256444591_Parent-child_communication
_during_adolescence/links/00b7d5229e56352c31000000
/Parent-child-communication-during-adolescence.pdf.

McLanahan, Sara, and Julia Adams. "Parenthood and Psychological
Well-Being." *Annual Review of Sociology,* August 1987.
AnnualReviews.org/doi/abs/10.1146/annurev.so.13.080187.001321.

Meier, Ann, Kelly Musick, Jocelyn Fischer, and Sarah Flood. "Mothers' and Fathers' Well-Being in Parenting Across the Arch of Child Development." *Journal of Marriage and Family.* US National Library of Medicine, August 2018. NCBI.NLM .NIH.gov/pmc/articles/PMC6136658.

Nomaguchi, Kei M., and Melissa A. Milkie. "Costs and Rewards of Children: The Effects of Becoming a Parent on Adults' Lives." Wiley Online Library. John Wiley & Sons, Ltd, February 19, 2004. OnlineLibrary.Wiley.com/doi/abs/10.1111/j.1741 -3737.2003.00356.x.

Raffaelli, Marcela, Karen Bogenschneider, and Mary Fran Flood. "Parent-Teen Communication About Sexual Topics." Faculty Publications, Department of Psychology. Digital Commons @ University of Nebraska–Lincoln, May 1998. DigitalCommons .UNL.edu/cgi/viewcontent.cgi?article=1097&context =psychfacpub.

CHAPTER 4

McCreary, Joedy. "Study: Black Drivers in NC Pulled over More than Twice as Often as White Drivers." CBS17.com, August 5, 2020. CBS17.com/news/north-carolina-news/study-black -drivers-in-nc-pulled over more than-twice-as-often-as -white-drivers.

Shroff, Ravi. "Research Shows Black Drivers More Likely to Be Stopped by Police." NYU Web Communications, May 5, 2020. NYU.edu/about/news-publications/news/2020/may/black -drivers-more-likely-to-be-stopped-by-police.html.

Sierra, Stephanie, and Lindsey Feingold. "Black Men Are 8 Times More Likely to Be Stopped by Oakland Police than White Men, Data Shows." ABC7 San Francisco. KGO-TV, September 9, 2020. ABC7News.com/oakland-police-opd-racial-profiling-traffic -stops/6414305.

Theran, Sally A. "Authenticity in Relationships and Depressive Symptoms: A Gender Analysis." *Personality and Individual Differences*. Pergamon, May 11, 2011. ScienceDirect.com/science/article/abs/pii/S0191886911001905.

CHAPTER 5

Clough, Sharice, and Melissa C. Duff. "The Role of Gesture in Communication and Cognition: Implications for Understanding and Treating Neurogenic Communication Disorders." *Frontiers in Human Neuroscience*, July 21, 2020. Frontiersin.org/articles/10.3389/fnhum.2020.00323/full.

Damour, Lisa. "What Do Teenagers Want? Potted Plant Parents." *New York Times*, December 14, 2016. NYTimes.com/2016/12/14/well/family/what-do-teenagers-want-potted-plant-parents.html?smid=tw-share.

Duck, Steve, and David T. McMahan. *Communication in Everyday Life: A Survey of Communication*. Thousand Oaks, CA: Sage Publications, Inc., 2021.

Emerson, Ralph Waldo. "The Conduct of Life." Gutenberg. Project Gutenberg, May 28, 2012. Gutenberg.org/files/39827/39827-h/39827-h.html.

Frank, Mark G., Darrin J. Griffin, Elena Svetiva, and Andreas Maroulis. "Nonverbal Elements of Voice." *The Social Psychology of Nonverbal Communication*. Springer Sociology, 2015. Link.Springer.com/chapter/10.1057/9781137345868_5.

CHAPTER 6

Barendse, Marjolein E. A., Theresa W. Cheng, and Jennifer H. Pfeifer. "Your Brain on Puberty." *Frontiers for Young Minds*, April 30, 2020. Kids.Frontiersin.org/articles/10.3389/frym.2020.00053.

Brookshire, Bethany. "Hormone Affects How Teens' Brains Control Emotions." *Science News for Students*, December 3, 2019. ScienceNewsForStudents.org/article/hormone-affects-how-teens-brains-control-emotions.

Davis, Matthew. "Hormones and the Adolescent Brain." BrainFacts .org. Accessed July 8, 2021. BrainFacts.org/thinking-sensing-and-behaving/childhood-and-adolescence/2015/hormones-and-the-adolescent-brain-120915.

Heatherton, Todd F. "Neuroscience of Self and Self-Regulation." *Annual Review of Psychology*. US National Library of Medicine, 2011. NCBI.NLM.NIH.gov/pmc/articles/PMC3056504.

Johns Hopkins Medicine. "Brain Anatomy and How the Brain Works." Accessed July 8, 2021. HopkinsMedicine.org/health/conditions-and-diseases/anatomy-of-the-brain.

Kabotyanski, Katherine E., and Leah H. Somerville. "Puberty: Your Brain on Hormones." *Frontiers for Young Minds*. Accessed July 8, 2021. Kids.Frontiersin.org/articles/10.3389/frym .2020.554380.

Moskowitz, Clara. "Teen Brains Clear Out Childhood Thoughts." *LiveScience*. March 23, 2009. LiveScience.com/3435-teen-brains-clear-childhood-thoughts.html.

Penttila, Nicky. "Beyond Raging Hormones." *Cerebrum*. Dana Foundation, September 6, 2019. Dana.org/article/beyond-raging-hormones.

Perlman, Susan B., and Kevin A. Pelphrey. "Regulatory Brain Development: Balancing Emotion and Cognition." *Social Neuroscience*. US National Library of Medicine, 2010. NCBI.NLM .NIH.gov/pmc/articles/PMC2950223.

Sakai, Jill. "Core Concept: How Synaptic Pruning Shapes Neural Wiring During Development and, Possibly, in Disease." *PNAS.* National Academy of Sciences, July 14, 2020. PNAS.org /content/117/28/16096.

Sisk, Cheryl L. "Development: Pubertal Hormones Meet the Adolescent Brain." *Current Biology.* Cell Press, July 24, 2017. ScienceDirect.com/science/article/pii/S0960982217307005.

Spear, Linda Patia. "Adolescent Neurodevelopment." *The Journal of Adolescent Health: Official Publication of the Society for Adolescent Medicine.* US National Library of Medicine, February 2013. NCBI.NLM.NIH.gov/pmc/articles/PMC3982854.

ZERO TO THREE. "When Does the Fetus's Brain Begin to Work?" Accessed July 8, 2021. ZeroToThree.org/resources/1375-when -does-the-fetus-s-brain-begin-to-work.

INDEX

ACKNOWLEDGMENTS

Thank you to the team at Rockridge Press and particularly my editors Jed Bickman and Caryn Abramowitz for the opportunity and support.

To the parents and teens who generously shared their stories with me so that I could use them to help other families. I am so grateful to you!

To friends and colleagues who offered support in real life and texts with food, memes, feedback, encouragement, walks, and hugs, thank you so much!

Huge thanks to my mom who, besides being an awesome mom in all ways, also read and provided helpful editing for this book, despite having her own deadlines and life to juggle.

Finally, thanks to Travis, Maggie, and Caroline for your love and support, patience and forgiveness, and making this project possible. I love you!

ABOUT THE AUTHOR

 **Katie Malinski**, LCSW-S, is an Austin-based parenting coach and therapist. With over 20 years' experience, Katie helps parents see the key connections that help resolve family difficulties, strengthen the parent–child relationship, and get families back on balance and moving forward together. Working with parents online and in-person, Katie offers individualized parent coaching and classes covering a broad spectrum of topics, including managing difficult behavior, parenting through divorce, and communicating about sexuality. Katie's calling—and passion—is improving family lives by offering understanding, a fresh perspective, and hope. Learn more about her approach, services, and workshops at ParenthoodUnderstood.com.

CPSIA information can be obtained
at www.ICGtesting.com
Printed in the USA
JSHW040449290122
22364JS00003B/6